HUTTON AND BUTLER

LIFTING THE LID ON
THE WORKINGS OF POWER

A British Academy Occasional Paper

HUTTON AND BUTLER

Lifting the Lid on the Workings of Power

EDITED BY

W. G. RUNCIMAN

Published for THE BRITISH ACADEMY

by OXFORD UNIVERSITY PRESS

Oxford University Press, Great Clarendon Street, Oxford OX2 6DP

Oxford New York
Auckland Bangkok Buenos Aires Cape Town Chennai
Dar es Salaam Delhi Hong Kong Istanbul Karachi Kolkata
Kuala Lumpur Madrid Melbourne Mexico City Mumbai Nairobi
São Paulo Shanghai Singapore Taipei Tokyo Toronto

Published in the United States
by Oxford University Press Inc., New York

© The British Academy 2004

Database right The British Academy (maker)

First published 2004
Reprinted 2005

British Library Cataloguing in Publication Data
Data available

ISBN 0–19–726329–1

Typeset in the offices of the British Academy
Printed in Great Britain
on acid-free paper by
Antony Rowe Limited
Chippenham, Wiltshire

Contents

Notes on Contributors   vii

Preface   ix

1.   What We Know Now   1
          W. G. Runciman

2.   The Hutton Inquiry: Some Wider Legal Aspects   29
          William Twining
          Discussion   51
            Michael Beloff

3.   The Lightning Flash on the Road to Baghdad:
          Issues of Evidence   61
            Peter Hennessy
          Discussion   82
            Richard Wilson

4.   Accuracy, Independence, and Trust   87
            Onora O'Neill
          Discussion   110
            John Lloyd

5.   Lessons for Governmental Process   115
            Michael Quinlan

Notes on Contributors

W. G. RUNCIMAN (Lord Runciman) is a Fellow of Trinity College, Cambridge, and President of the British Academy. He chaired the Royal Commission on Criminal Justice in England and Wales of 1991–93.

WILLIAM TWINING QC is Research Professor of Law at University College London, and a Fellow of the British Academy.

MICHAEL BELOFF QC is President of Trinity College, Oxford, and a Judge of the Court of Appeal of Jersey and Guernsey.

PETER HENNESSY is Attlee Professor of Contemporary British History at Queen Mary, London, and a Fellow of the British Academy.

RICHARD WILSON (Lord Wilson of Dinton) is Master of Emmanuel College, Cambridge. He was Secretary of the Cabinet from 1998 to 2002.

ONORA O'NEILL (Baroness O'Neill) is Principal of Newnham College, Cambridge, and President-elect of the British Academy.

JOHN LLOYD is Editor of the *Financial Times* magazine.

SIR MICHAEL QUINLAN was Permanent Under-Secretary of State at the Ministry of Defence from 1988 to 1992, and Director of the Ditchley Foundation from 1992 to 1999.

Preface

This volume originates from the proceedings of a public meeting organized by the British Academy on 'Hutton — the Wider Issues' which was held at Chatham House, London on 19 July 2004. Since Lord Butler's *Review of Intelligence on Weapons of Mass Destruction* had been published a few days before, the speakers and discussants were able to take account of it too in their presentations, and this volume does likewise. The purpose of the meeting was explicitly not to challenge Lord Hutton's account of the sequence of events which led up to the tragic death of Dr David Kelly, but to consider, under the three headings of 'Law', 'Evidence', and 'Trust', some of the questions about public policy, the conduct of government business, and the relations between government, media, and public which the Hutton Report had raised. The views expressed by the three principal speakers and myself, all of whom are Fellows of the Academy, are our own, as are those of the discussants and of Sir Michael Quinlan, who generously agreed to contribute a concluding essay. But the volume will, I hope, serve to demonstrate something of what the British Academy can do to promote non-partisan discussion about current events which are of exceptional interest to academic researchers and the general public alike.

On behalf of the Academy, I would like to express thanks not only to all the contributors, but also to the members of the Academy's staff who helped to make the meeting a success and to James Rivington, the Academy's Publications Officer, and his staff for their help in seeing this volume through to publication.

W. G. R.

What We Know Now

W. G. RUNCIMAN

Introduction

Nothing revealed in either the Hutton Report or the Butler Report is going to bring to agreement those who, on the one side, believe that Tony Blair was right to join Britain with the United States in overturning Saddam Hussein by force whether there were weapons of mass destruction (WMD) to be found in Iraq or not and those who, on the other side, would have continued to regard the invasion as both imprudent and illegal even if such weapons had been found in the way that Blair so over-confidently predicted that they would. But nobody who has read the two reports can fail to conclude that the Government, the intelligence services, and the BBC all fell short to some degree of what might have been hoped, or even expected, of them at a time when the country was on the brink of being taken into a war.

Whether, in this instance, that makes any of the protagonists morally culpable or whether, on the contrary, to understand is to forgive, is up to you. To the non-participant and (so far as possible) non-partisan academic observer, the questions most interestingly posed by the disclosures in the two reports are not who behaved well and who badly, so much as who, by their behaviour, made how much difference to what did and didn't happen; not whether this was a just or an unjust war, so much as whether it was publicly justified for reasons which dissolve under scrutiny; not whether Lords Hutton and Butler ought or ought not to have agreed to the terms of reference given to them, so much as what were the implications of their having done so; and not whether either journalists or politicians are entitled to present to the public as facts things which they cannot be certain are true, so much as what consequences follow from their seeing it as their right, or even duty, to do so.

Decisions and how they were taken

It is by now generally accepted that Tony Blair's mind had been made up about Iraq some time before final decisions were taken. As Alastair Campbell wrote in his minute to John Scarlett of 17 November 2002, 'he is not exactly a "don't know" on the issue';[1] and as Blair himself told the Butler Committee, 'what changed for me with September 11th was that I thought then you have to change your mindset … you have to go out and get after the different aspects of this threat'.[2] It is also, since the Butler Report, generally accepted that this 'had the result that more weight was placed on the intelligence than it could bear.'[3] To the more strenuous opponents of the war, like Professor Conor Gearty, the conclusion which follows is that Blair must have been either 'mad' (i.e. he had a totally unreasonable belief in the existence of WMD), 'bad' (i.e. he lied about them to fool the country into war), or 'had' (i.e. he was tricked by the intelligence community).[4] But the final version of the celebrated dossier of 24 September 2002 was both fully and unanimously endorsed by the Joint Intelligence Committee (JIC), and no evidence has come to light which would endorse the view that its members were putting their names to a document which contained information which they knew to be untrue. Their failure, as we know now, was that they did not do enough either to guard against the possibility that their

---

[1] Lord Hutton, *Report of the Inquiry into the Circumstances Surrounding the Death of David Kelly C.M.G.*, HC 247 (Stationery Office, 28 January 2004) (hereafter Hutton), p. 133

[2] *Review of Intelligence on Weapons of Mass Destruction. Report of a Committee of Privy Counsellors*, HC 898 (Stationery Office, 14 July 2004) (hereafter Butler), p. 63.

[3] Butler p. 114.

[4] *London Review of Books*, 19 February 2004.

information might be seriously unreliable, or to make sure that it was not presented in such a way as to make it appear more reliable than it was. How could an intelligence service staffed by skilled professionals of long experience not have seen to it that its reservations about the quality of the information underlying the judgements which it passed on to Government were made clear? And how could a democratic Government concerned by its prospective need to justify to the electorate a decision to invade a foreign state not have ensured that it could, in that event, demonstrate beyond reasonable doubt that the threat posed by the ruler of that state was as serious as the Prime Minister had claimed?[5]

Both these questions are given added force by what we know now from Dr Brian Jones.[6] On 30 May 2003 David Kelly told Susan Watts, Science Editor of BBC *Newsnight*, that 'it was very difficult to get comments in because people at the top of the ladder didn't want to hear some of the things',[7] and Hutton reveals that when Dr Jones, having returned from holiday on 18 September 2002, voiced concerns which, as his superiors subsequently confirmed,[8] he had every right to do, they were not transmitted to the Chairman of the JIC. Nor was Dr Jones invited to give an

---

[5] The Chairman of the JIC, John Scarlett, told the Butler Committee that the dossier was in no sense, in his mind or in the mind of the JIC, 'a document designed to make a case for anything' (Butler p. 78). This is accepted by Butler to the extent of agreeing that it was 'not intended to make a case for a particular course of action' but 'to gain support for the general direction in which Government policy had been moving … away from containment to a more proactive approach to enforcing Iraqi disarmament'. I return to this point later on.

[6] Head of the nuclear, chemical and biological weapons section in the Scientific and Technical Directorate of the Defence Intelligence Analysis Staff.

[7] Hutton p. 17.

[8] Hutton p. 125; Butler pp. 137–8.

assessment of the material from the new (and questionable) source which was incorporated into the dossier.[9] The Deputy Chief of Defence Intelligence told Lord Hutton that 'it was not necessary to raise the issue with Mr Scarlett'[10] on the grounds that he was sure that Scarlett would have asked what was his, and the Chief of Defence Intelligence's, view; and the Chief of Defence Intelligence told Lord Butler that 'I saw it as part of the day-to-day process' — a remark which is left to stand without further comment on the grounds that 'It is not our intention in this report to revisit issues already addressed by Lord Hutton.'[11] But the Butler Report does, of course, revisit issues already addressed by Lord Hutton, as it could hardly fail to do; and it is the Butler Report which tells us that 'the exclusion of Brian Jones and his staff from readership of the original report meant that this intelligence was not seen by the few people in the UK intelligence community able to form all-round, professional technical judgements on its reliability and significance.'[12] What is more, 'the SIS [Secret Intelligence Service] withdrew the intelligence from this source as unreliable in July 2003.'

All this is no doubt regrettable. But how surprising is it? And what difference would it have made if the JIC *had* been party to Dr Jones's legitimate and (as we know now) justifiable concerns? He would have been likely to have come straight up against what might be called the 'Arnhem Effect': in 1944, the decision to go 'a bridge too far' was taken despite last-minute aerial-photographic intelligence showing that the German resistance which would be

---

[9] Butler p. 138.

[10] Hutton p. 125. Mr Tony Cragg was Deputy Chief of Defence Intelligence at the time the dossier was prepared.

[11] Butler p. 137. Air Marshal Sir Joe French was Chief of Defence Intelligence at the time the dossier was prepared.

[12] Butler p. 138.

encountered would be much stronger than previously believed. But who was going to call the whole long-planned operation off on that account? In the present case, it is not new intelligence but well-founded doubts about both old and, more particularly, one new source of intelligence which is at issue. But the point is the same. How plausible is it to suppose that if Dr Jones's views had been aired as they should have been among the 'people at the top of the ladder', Britain would not have joined in the invasion of Iraq? The military and logistic preparations are known to have been in place, and although mobilization does not necessarily commit a Government to going to war it is difficult to imagine minds being changed at the very last minute by doubts about one source of intelligence that was being used to bolster the Government's case. In fact, the Chief of SIS, Dr Richard Dearlove, told the Butler Committee that he had, in the course of briefing Blair on Iraq on 12 September 2002, told him that the new intelligence source, potentially important as it was, 'remained unproven'.[13] So a whiff of doubt did reach the top of the ladder after all, however little effect it had when it had got there.

Perhaps, therefore, the more intriguing question to ask is not how the Prime Minister's mind could have been changed, but how inappropriate credence came to be given to an unreliable intelligence source. And this takes us back to what Hutton reveals about the pressure put on the JIC by Downing Street. The Government's decision to use the JIC to prepare a document to be used for the public presentation of policy was, as the Butler Committee notes, unprecedented. But its reason for doing so is very clear: 'The advantage to the Government of associating the JIC's name with the dossier was the badge of objectivity that it brought with it and the credibility which this would give to the

---

[13] Butler p. 139.

document.'[14] This, as Alastair Campbell made clear to John Scarlett, required ownership of the document to lie, and be seen to lie, with the JIC,[15] and Scarlett accepted it.[16] But as Hutton puts it, in a careful concessive clause, 'it is clear that 10 Downing Street took a close interest in the drafting of the dossier'.[17] Scarlett was left in no doubt, as the exchanges reproduced by Hutton make clear, that the Prime Minister wished the JIC to present its case as strongly as was consistent — whatever exactly that means in this context — with the information it had; and Butler confirms this. Lord Hutton, in a phrase which has attracted a good deal of comment, says that this 'may have subconsciously influenced Mr Scarlett and the other members of the JIC to make the wording of the dossier somewhat stronger than it would have been if it had been contained in a normal JIC assessment.'[18] But the members of the JIC must have been only too conscious of the position in which they had been placed. Nobody serving on such a body can be so unsophisticated as not to be aware that the line between presentation and content is not an easy one to draw. In a situation as delicate as this one, could the JIC not be expected to be more, rather than less, concerned to hold fast to the distinction (in the words that Butler uses) between assessment and advocacy?

---

[14] Butler p. 78.

[15] Hutton p. 108.

[16] Hutton p. 110. At a meeting held on 18 September 2002, however, it was, on Scarlett's testimony (Hutton p. 111) 'immediately agreed that this was a document that was going to be presented — or since this was a document that was going to be presented by the Prime Minister to Parliament on behalf of the Government, its ownership, in that sense, looking ahead to that moment, lay with No.10 and the JIC itself does not produce documents for public dissemination and there had never been any intention that it would do so.'

[17] Hutton p. 141.

[18] Hutton p. 320.

The assessment of intelligence, as numerous commentators have pointed out, is a complex and often tortuous exercise in which certainty is elusive, blind alleys commonplace, and even the most apparently reliable sources can turn out to be nothing of the kind. 'Intelligence', Blair himself conceded in the House of Commons on 24 September 2002, 'is not always right', before going on to ask rhetorically whether, 'with what we know and what we can reasonably speculate' the world would be 'wise to leave the present situation undisturbed'. But speculation, however reasonable, might be thought a questionably sufficient justification for taking the country into a pre-emptive war, whether legitimized or not by reference to United Nations Security Council resolutions 678, 687, and 1441. Would it not have been a reasonable speculation that no British Government would take such a decision without substantially more reliable evidence about the threat posed by Saddam Hussein than was in fact forthcoming, and that the JIC would have ensured that its tradition which (so the Butler Committee was 'assured by all witnesses') had hitherto 'prevented policy imperatives from dominating objective assessment'[19] was more, not less, firmly upheld? Butler draws the conclusion that there is 'a strong case for the post of Chairman of the JIC being held by someone with experience of dealing with Ministers in a very senior role, and who is demonstrably beyond influence, and thus probably in his last post'[20] — an unmistakable hint that John Scarlett could have been all too consciously influenced by an awareness that compliance with the Prime Minister's known wishes might not be unhelpful to his subsequent career. Again, there is nothing surprising in this. Such inducements are a familiar part of (to borrow the phrase of the Chief of Defence Intelligence) the 'day-to-day process' of institutional and political life. But

---

[19] Butler p. 144.
[20] Butler p. 144.

whether or not a different Chairman of the JIC would have acted differently, Butler leaves us with the inescapable conclusion that what actually happened was that on an occasion when it was more, not less, important that the JIC 'should, where there are significant limitations in the intelligence, state these clearly',[21] that is what the JIC did *not* do. The consequence was that the Prime Minister was able to say to the House of Commons on 24 September 2002 that the picture which the intelligence sources had given to him was 'extensive, detailed and authoritative' when, as we know now, it was not.

Was there anybody else who could have prevented this from happening? Not, it would appear, the members of the Cabinet. They 'were offered and many received briefings on the intelligence picture on Iraq.'[22] But whatever those briefings contained, they did not contain the doubts and caveats which had not even reached the Chairman of the JIC. We also know now from Butler that although, as Peter Hennessy also highlights,[23] 'excellent quality papers' had been written by officials, they were not discussed in Cabinet where the frequent briefings, whether given by the Prime Minister, the Foreign Secretary, or the Defence Secretary, were oral and unscripted. Again, there is nothing surprising in this, given what is already well known about the style of Government under Blair. Nor, in any case, is Blair the first, nor will he be the last, Prime Minister to bypass officials when it suits him, or to limit collective discussion in Cabinet, or to hire a hardened professional to bully the media, or to rely on a small group of key ministers, selected officials, and political advisers dependent on his personal patronage. Butler does, however, point out that the unprecedented use of the JIC to put its name to a document to be used in support

---

[21] Butler p. 146.
[22] Butler p. 147.
[23] See below, p. 73.

of public presentation of the Government's case was in the context of two changes in the machinery of Government which had implications for the application of intelligence to collective ministerial decision-making: the splitting of the responsibility of the Cabinet Secretary through the redefinition of the post of Security and Intelligence Co-ordinator, and the combination of the posts of Head of the Defence and Overseas Secretariat and Head of the European Affairs Secretariat with the posts of the Prime Minister's advisers on Foreign Affairs and European Affairs respectively.[24] It must therefore be possible, and may even be likely, that a Cabinet Secretary with the support and authority that Cabinet Secretaries used to enjoy would not only have been able to see to it that the Cabinet was more fully and impartially briefed than this Cabinet was, but would also have prevented the JIC from being placed by the Prime Minister and his personal advisers in the position in which this Prime Minister and his personal advisers deliberately placed it. We cannot be sure. But we do know now that the decision to go to war was taken without the extent of informed discussion in Cabinet that would have been normal in the past.

So the dossier was published, the country went to war, Andrew Gilligan[25] met Dr David Kelly in the Charing Cross Hotel on 22 May 2003, and Gilligan gave the unscripted interview on the *Today* programme which his superiors defended against the attacks of Alastair Campbell[26] without, as we know now, taking what might be thought the rudimentary precaution of going through Gilligan's notes to make sure that they adequately substantiated the claim which he had made that 'actually the

---

[24] Butler p. 147.

[25] Defence and diplomatic correspondent of the *Today* programme on BBC Radio 4.

[26] The Prime Minister's Director of Communications and Strategy.

government probably … knew that that forty five minute figure was wrong, even before it decided to put it in.'[27] How could Greg Dyke, Director-General of the BBC, have failed to see what damage Gilligan might have done, and failed to brief himself adequately on what had actually been said and by whom? There is an unhappy symmetry between the failure of the JIC and the BBC alike to check their sources in a way that the importance of the issues involved might lead an outside observer to presume that they would have made sure to do.

But there is a seeming asymmetry too. Neither the JIC nor the BBC checked their sources as carefully as they should. But where the Chairman of the JIC is subsequently promoted by the Prime Minister, both the Director-General of the BBC and the Chairman of its Governors are compelled to resign. Should we conclude that a double standard has been at work? Butler goes out of his way to argue that demands for John Scarlett's resignation should be resisted. But he does severely criticize the way in which intelligence on Iraq was 'analysed and assessed … and then incorporated into JIC assessments for Ministers and other senior readers.'[28] If the Chairman of the BBC is ultimately responsible for management failures down the line, does the same not apply to a Prime Minister who is being charged, in the words applied by John Kerry to George Bush, with having not led so much as *mis*led his country into war? But Blair had no reason whatever to resign unless he was found to have deceived the House of Commons — that is, to have justified his decision to go to war by asserting as known to be true what he himself knew to be false — and both Hutton and Butler believe that he did not. He was not going to have to resign because he overestimated his influence with Bush and underestimated Chirac's disdain for himself, or because two

---

[27] Hutton p. 12.
[28] Butler p. 109.

million people in Britain turned out for 'stop the war' rallies, or because Robin Cook knew of nothing which led to the conclusion that Saddam had weapons which posed a threat to Britain, or because Clare Short thought he was straining the loyalty of the Labour Party, or because without a further UN resolution Britain might lose a case before the International Court of Justice, or even because 139 Labour MPs rebelled against him. It is true that the terms of reference given to both Hutton and Butler were tightly circumscribed, as they were bound to be. But they were not such as to preclude the possibility of their finding out something which would have called the Prime Minister's integrity into serious question. Lord Hutton was well aware that 'a number of public figures and commentators'[29] thought that his terms of reference entitled, if not required, him to address the question whether the intelligence in relation to WMD set out in the dossier was of sufficient strength and reliability to justify the Government in deciding that Iraq under Saddam Hussein posed such a threat to the safety and interests of the United Kingdom that military action should be taken. He declined to do so. But even before it was supplemented by the evidence made public by Lord Butler, the evidence made public by Hutton gave the Government's opponents plentiful grounds on which to argue that the answer is no.

The topic to which that inevitably leads on is the weakness in Parliament of the Prime Minister's critics. Blair's indisputable success in stealing the Conservatives' clothes had placed him in a position where his most irate opponents were either Liberal Democrats, who could safely be discounted, or his own back-benchers (former ministers included) who, however resentful of what they might see as his abandonment or even betrayal of

---

[29] Hutton p. 2.

principles for which the Labour Party had traditionally stood, were not going to go into the lobby against him on a vote of confidence called by the Opposition. Whether or not the tactics of Michael Howard as Leader of the Opposition were as ill-chosen as some newspapers portrayed them, no Conservative leader was going to be able to exploit the Hutton and Butler reports in the way that a Labour Opposition might have been able to do if a Conservative Government, in alliance with as right-wing an American government as this one, had taken the country to war in the same way. The effective opposition was therefore left to the media. But the BBC, through being over-concerned — rightly, as Hutton agreed[30] — to protect its independence against Alastair Campbell's attacks, handed victory to their enemy on a plate.

We shall never know what would and wouldn't have happened if David Kelly had not decided to talk to Andrew Gilligan. But two remarks made by Kelly to Susan Watts on 30 May 2003 do, in the light of what we know now, stand out on the page.[31] First, 'on the 45 minutes' (SW), 'oh that I knew because I knew the concern about the statement ... it was a statement that was made and it just got out of all proportion ... you know someone ... They were desperate for information ... they were pushing hard for information which could be released ... that was one that popped up and it was seized on ... and it was unfortunate that it was ... which is why there is the argument between the intelligence services and cabinet office/number ten, because things were picked up on, and once they've picked up on it you can't pull it back, that's the problem ...'. Second, in answer to 'do you think there ought to be a security and intelligence committee enquiry?' (SW), 'yes but not now. I think that has to be done in about six

---

[30] Hutton p. 322.

[31] The entire conversation as tape-recorded is reproduced by Hutton in an Appendix (Hutton pp. 339–44).

months time when we actually have come to the end of the evaluation of Iraq and the information that is going to come out of it.'

Words and word-smithing

As David Kelly also said to Susan Watts in the course of that same conversation, 'you know the word-smithing is actually quite important'.[32] He could hardly have said a truer word. Lord Hutton, having remarked that 'The term "sexed-up" is a slang expression, the meaning of which lacks clarity in the context of the dossier', concluded that the 'sexing-up' allegation was unfounded because 'it would have been understood by those who heard the broadcasts to mean that the dossier had been embellished with intelligence known or believed to be false or unreliable, which was not the case', as opposed to being so drafted as 'to make the case against Saddam Hussain as strong as the intelligence contained in it permitted'.[33] But what does 'embellishment' mean? Lord Hutton knows as well as any barrister who has appeared before him that advocacy is all about deciding what evidence to include or exclude, particularly making sure not to include anything *known* to be false or unreliable. What about omitting 'caveats'?[34] Or about 'emphasis' which 'went too far'?[35] Or 'more assertive'?[36] Or about the suspicions, implicitly endorsed by Butler, that the '45 minute'

---

[32] Hutton p. 341.
[33] Hutton p. 153.
[34] Hutton p. 15; Butler p. 80.
[35] Susan Watts in Hutton p. 23.
[36] Hutton p. 37.

report from the classified assessment had been repeated in the dossier 'because of its eye-catching character'?[37]

All this might be held to give Andrew Gilligan grounds to argue in his defence that the dossier *had* been strengthened in its wording to the point of being 'sexed up' and that the evidence which Hutton and Butler have brought to light supports him. But Gilligan had committed the irreparable mistake, to which he subsequently had to admit,[38] of attributing to David Kelly opinions which were not David Kelly's but his own. Michael Beloff[39] argues that the BBC and others must be free to report, although not of course 'recklessly', 'potentially false accusations of fact impugning the integrity of others including politicians'. But he goes on to say that the law cannot allow untruths to be disseminated simply on the basis that they have been told by someone else, and Gilligan made a serious allegation which he couldn't substantiate and attributed to somebody who had not in fact made it.

On the other hand, suppose that the BBC had broadcast no more and no less than that there were experts within the intelligence services charged with assessing Saddam Hussein's ability and readiness to deploy WMD who were concerned that the Government was placing too much reliance on questionable intelligence but were unable to make their concerns known at as high a level of decision-making as they would have wished. In that event, it is difficult to suppose that either Gavyn Davies or Greg Dyke, let alone both of them, would not still be in their jobs as Chairman and Director-General of the BBC. Michael Beloff's word 'recklessly' is itself a contestable one — how reckless is 'reckless'? — and perhaps it would still have been reckless of the BBC to broadcast an allegation by an unnamed source which implied that

---

[37] Butler p. 127.
[38] Hutton pp. 164–5.
[39] See below, pp. 57–8.

16

ministers and officials were deliberately preventing expert judgement on the value of information on which the government was going to rely in making a case for going to war from reaching 'people at the top of the ladder'. Might Alastair Campbell still have been able to sustain the charge that the BBC had made a serious and unsubstantiated allegation 'damaging to the integrity of the Prime Minister, the Government, and the political process'?[40] Perhaps. But it looks unlikely that he would have thought it necessary,[41] and even if he had, and the BBC had stood by a story based on information which Dr Brian Jones subsequently confirmed, and Butler endorsed, Campbell could still have played the card that the Chief of the SIS did tell the Prime Minister on 12 September 2002 that the new source 'remained unproven'. This, to be sure, does not alter the fact that the JIC was not given the benefit of the professional judgement of the members of the intelligence service best qualified to provide it. But a broadcast to that effect would not have provoked the 'rumpus', as Susan Watts called it, that Gilligan did.

There is, however, more to word-smithing than choice of words. There is also omission to make clear how the chosen words are to be construed where there is room for doubt. Not the least intriguing of the things we know now is the wilful non-correction of the ambiguity about whether the 45-minute deployment referred to battlefield or strategic weapons. There was, on Scarlett's evidence, 'no discussion with the Prime Minister that I

---

[40] Hutton p. 691.

[41] Richard Sambrook (Director, BBC News), writing to Alastair Campbell on 27 June 2003, quotes several journalists whose contacts had already reported to them that intelligence reports were being exaggerated to strengthen the case against Saddam Hussein — or, as it had been put in the *Observer* on 24 February 2003, 'the essence of the disagreement is said to have been that intelligence material should be presented "straight" rather than *spiced* up [my italics] to make a political argument' (Hutton p. 694).

can recall about the 45 minutes point in connection with battlefield or strategic systems.'[42] But Sir Richard Dearlove, when confronted by the criticism made by the Foreign Affairs Committee about the importance given to the '45 minutes' claim, conceded that 'given the misinterpretation that was placed on the 45 minutes intelligence, with the benefit of hindsight you can say that is a valid criticism.'[43] Whatever the reason for which Blair, unlike his Foreign Secretary, didn't ask, and wasn't told, why it not only might be but was a misinterpretation to allege that the '45 minutes' claim referred to long-range weapons, the Prime Ministerial Foreword to the dossier asserted that 'the document discloses that [Saddam's] military planning allows for some of the WMD to be ready within 45 minutes of an order to use them.'[44] Once that had been said, it was only to be expected that the media would then pick it up.[45] But when they did, no Government source made any attempt to put them right. Perhaps that too was only to be expected. But when the Defence Secretary, Geoff Hoon, was cross-examined before Lord Hutton on 22 September 2003, his replies were so disarmingly revealing as to merit reproduction in full.[46]

---

[42] Hutton p. 150.

[43] Hutton p. 147.

[44] *Iraq's Weapons of Mass Destruction: The Assessment of the British Government* (Stationery Office, 24 September 2002), p. 4.

[45] In a footnote (Butler p. 127 n. 5), we are told that the Butler Committee asked 60 editors if they had been briefed by representatives of the Government about the dossier, and that all those who replied said they had not been guided to particular parts prior to its publication. But how many didn't reply, and what might they have said? Furthermore, there was 'some evidence' that 'some journalists had had their attention drawn *after* its publication to passages in the Prime Minister's Foreword'. Who these journalists were, and whether it was the '45 minute' WMD claim that was drawn to their attention, we are not told.

[46] Hutton pp. 148–50.

Q. Did you know that the 45 minute claim in the dossier was taken from a JIC assessment which does not in fact identify any particular weapon?

A. Well, I recall at the time having some discussion in the Ministry of Defence about the kinds of weapons that could be deployed within 45 minutes; and I think the assumption was made that they would be, for example, chemical shells, which were clearly capable of being deployed, as I think Mr Scarlett has indicated to the Inquiry, in a time even less than 45 minutes; I think he suggested 20 minutes.

Q. So you knew, did you, that the munitions referred to were only battlefield munitions?

A. I was certainly aware that that was one suggestion, yes.

Q. Was there any other suggestion that they were not battlefield munitions but strategic munitions?

A. I recall asking what kind of weapons would be deployable within 45 minutes; and the answer is the answer that I have just given to you.

Q. Which was shells, battlefield mortars, tactical weapons of that kind?

A. Yes.

Q. Would your Department be responsible for correcting any false impression given by the press on an issue of this importance?

A. I think on an issue of this importance it would not simply have been the Ministry of Defence that was solely responsible. There would have been an effort across Government.

Q. Are you aware that on 25th September a number of newspapers had banner headlines suggesting that this related to strategic missiles or bombs?

A. I can recall, yes.

Q. Why was no corrective statement issued for the benefit of the public in relation to those media reports?

A. I do not know.

Q. It must have been considered by someone, must it not?

A. I have spent many years trying to persuade newspapers and journalists to correct their stories. I have to say it is an extraordinarily time consuming and generally frustrating process.

Q. I am sorry, are you saying that the press would not report a corrective statement that the dossier was meant to refer, in this context, to battlefield munitions and not to strategic weapons?

A. What I am suggesting is that I was not aware of whether any consideration was given to such a correction. All that I do know from my experience is that, generally speaking, newspapers are resistant to corrections. That judgement may have been made by others as well.

Q. But, Mr Hoon, you must have been horrified that the dossier had been misrepresented in this way; it was a complete distortion of what it actually was intended to convey, was it not?

A. Well, I was not horrified. I recognised that journalists occasionally write things that are more dramatic than the material upon which it is based.

Q. Can we forget journalists for the moment and concentrate on the members of the public who are reading it? Will they not be entitled to be given the true picture of the intelligence, not a vastly inflated one?

A. I think that is a question you would have to put to the journalists and the editors responsible.

Q. But you had the means to correct it, not them. They could not correct it until they were told, could they?

A. Well, as I say, my experience of trying to persuade newspapers to correct false impressions is one that is not full of success.

Q. Do you accept that on this topic at least you had an absolute duty to try to correct it?

A. No, I do not.

Q. Do you accept that you had any duty to correct it?

A. Well, I apologise for repeating the same answer, but you are putting the question in another way. I have tried on many, many occasions to persuade journalists and newspapers to correct stories. They do not like to do so.

Q. Can I suggest to you a reason why this was not done? It would have been politically highly embarrassing because it would have revealed the dossier as published was at least highly capable of being misleading.

A. Well, I do not accept that.

Q. So your suggestion is that this was a disgraceful exaggeration by the press of what was clear in the dossier as a reference to battlefield munitions?

A. I am certainly suggesting that it was an exaggeration, but it is not unusual for newspapers to exaggerate.

Q. Can you tell me, if you happen to have it to hand, where in the dossier it is made clear that the CBW [chemical and biological] weapons which were the subject of the 45 minute claim were only battlefield munitions?

A. Well, I do not have it to hand; and I do not know whether it was made clear.

What are future historians likely to say about that riveting, not to say breathtaking, exchange? The Defence Secretary of a country which has gone to war on what its critics are alleging to be a false prospectus says that he made no attempt to correct an admitted misunderstanding about one of the reasons given by the Prime Minister for contemplating doing so, on the grounds that in his experience journalists are famously resistant to correcting their stories and he has not in the past had much success in getting them to do so. It is almost as if Geoff Hoon was inviting Lord Hutton and the rest of us to picture Alastair Campbell saying that he made no attempt to get Andrew Gilligan's broadcast corrected because journalists are so difficult to persuade to back down. Lord Hutton, again, makes clear that he regarded the distinction between battlefield and strategic weapons as falling outside his terms of reference.[47] But he nevertheless reprints the comment of the

---

[47] Hutton p. 145.

Intelligence and Security Committee, in its report presented to Parliament in September 2003, that the failure of the dossier to make it clear was 'unhelpful to an understanding of the issue' — a piece of word-smithing which takes understatement almost to the point of parody.

So are Hutton and Butler themselves wordsmiths who forged their chosen phrases with too much circumspection to have the right perlocutionary effect? To that question, the answer depends on who their audience is to be taken to be. To newspaper editors, whether broadsheet or tabloid, hoping for outspoken, headline-grabbing apportionment of guilt, the answer was always going to be yes. But metaphors like 'whitewash' or 'pulling punches' or 'cover-up' are not made any more appropriate on that account. The language of the law and the Civil Service, like that of science and scholarship, is often irritating, and understandably so, to readers to whom precision can seem like pedantry, even-handedness like pusillanimity, and elaborate syntax a symptom of gratuitous intellectual condescension. But reports like these will fail to achieve the purpose which their authors properly intend them to serve if they are not so worded as to make them equally difficult to discredit both for those who think they have gone too far and for those who think they have not gone far enough. Thanks to Hutton and Butler, we now know things about the workings of power in the run-up to the invasion of Iraq for which historians might otherwise have had to wait for decades, and it is up to their commentators, whether journalists, politicians, or academics, to use the evidence they have made available to draw conclusions which they have not chosen to draw themselves.

Disclosure and exposure

Butler concludes that 'if intelligence is to be used more widely by governments in public debate in the future, those doing so must be careful to explain its uses and limitations.'[48] Yes, indeed. John Scarlett, as we have seen,[49] denied that the dossier was designed to make a case for anything. But nobody can seriously suppose that it was designed to make a case for nothing. The Foreign Secretary told the Butler Committee that its purpose was to 'make a case for the world to recognise the importance of the issue and hopefully to galvanise the international community into taking it seriously',[50] and the Defence Secretary told them that 'if we were going to be able to make out a case for war against Iraq, we were going to have to publish the material.'[51] To suggest that the Government made the unprecedented use of the JIC for no other purpose than the disinterested disclosure to the public of information which might help them to make up their minds about Iraq is a little like saying that, when a sign is put up at a ski resort saying 'Danger of Avalanches', it is merely disclosing information which might help skiers to make up their minds about the weather, rather than warning them to keep off the slopes.

Once, however, the Government had decided to do what it did, it was inevitable that there would be some members of the intelligence services who would at least consider whether they ought to blow the whistle, with all the attendant risks which that might involve. Whatever Dr David Kelly's particular motives and expectations may have been, he was not alone. Even for civil servants with long experience of dealing with journalists, the

---

[48] Butler p. 115.
[49] See above n. 5.
[50] Butler p. 79.
[51] Butler p. 77.

decision to give an unauthorized interview on politically sensitive matters is fraught with hazard. But if a Government is seen at first hand by loyal and long-serving members of the intelligence services to be using intelligence in what they regard as an improperly tendentious way, it is not surprising that one or more of them should come to the conclusion that their duty to their service and to their country overrides their duty to the Prime Minister of the day.

Once that happens, it is going to be open season for scoop-hungry journalists for whom disclosure of confidential information is to be welcomed in direct proportion to its potential for naming persons in positions of power who can be exposed as having done, or failed to do, something which they hoped to conceal. As happens in all arms races, both literal and metaphorical, the cleverer the spinners become at spinning, the cleverer the unravellers become at unravelling, and the cleverer the spinners become at re-spinning what the unravellers have unravelled. If Peter Hennessy is right, ministers and officials will be as unwilling after Iraq to 'do a Tony' as they were after Suez to 'do an Anthony'. But if another Government does again provoke unease within the intelligence services of the same kind and for the same reasons as the Blair Government is now known to have done over Iraq, its members will have only themselves to blame if it generates a similar cycle of resistance to spin leading to blowing of whistles leading to media intrusion leading to a reimposition of a tradition of confidentiality which had been relaxed by the Government for a particular purpose of its own.

It may be too obvious to need saying that a Secret Intelligence Service can hardly be expected to perform the function for which it was created once it ceases to be secret. But in open, liberal, democratic societies such as both Britain and the United States are represented by their Governments as being, neither MI6 nor the CIA can expect to be impenetrably screened from enquiry by either sceptical politicians or intrusive journalists, or both. There is no way of resolving to the satisfaction of all involved the perennial dilemma of reconciling the public's wish to know something about what the country's intelligence services are doing and the intelligence services' wish to keep secret things whose disclosure would undermine their ability to do it. But a Government suspected, whether rightly or wrongly, of using the intelligence services to influence public opinion for purposes which the public will not necessarily endorse cannot complain if its reasonable speculations, to echo Tony Blair's own phrase, are countered by the reasonable speculations of sceptical politicians and intrusive journalists. Journalists cannot, any more than Governments themselves, be absolutely sure that their speculations, however reasonable, are well-founded. But are they not entitled to feel that they have what might be called the right of non-reckless conjecture? Just how that right is to be defined is then a matter to be settled in due course by custom, precedent, the decisions of the courts, and the conclusions drawn by both sides in the continuing arms race from what is revealed in reports like those of Lord Hutton and Lord Butler.

Conclusion

It is too soon to predict what the so-called verdict of history will be on an episode about which there is much still to find out beyond what was disclosed to either Hutton or Butler. But the historians of the future will surely have a lot to say about Blair himself, and it is unlikely that they will be any more unanimous about him than the vociferous writers of letters to the newspapers of the present day. To his detractors, he will continue to be an unappealing combination of sanctimoniousness, hubris, and naivety; to his admirers, he will continue to be the 'regular guy' that he claims to be whose personal and political skills turned 'New' Labour into a triumphantly re-electable party of government; and to the weary cynics of *Realpolitik* for whom there are neither heroes nor villains, he will continue to be another ambitious politician propelled by the accident of his predecessor's death into a position of leadership where, like the rest of them, he soon learned how to sup with the devil and moved predictably further away from his one-time professed ideals.

For the present, however, it is of less interest how many readers of the Hutton and Butler reports fall into one rather than another of those three categories, than how much Blair may have forfeited the trust of voters who had previously given him the benefit of the doubt. Tempting as it is to draw parallels with the position of Eden after Suez, the differences are enough to make the parallels less instructive than they may initially appear. Even if you continue to suspect that not only Eden but also Blair misled Parliament and the country by refusing to admit that a decision to go to war had been taken when in fact it had, Eden's invasion of Egypt was a war of his own making which the Americans could not be guaranteed to support, whereas Blair's war was an invasion of Iraq on which the Americans had decided and which, as US Secretary of Defense Donald Rumsfeld made embarrassingly clear, the British could join or not as the British Prime Minister might decide. Whatever losses of men and material British forces might suffer, however many innocent Iraqi civilians might be maimed or killed, and however incapable the Coalition might turn out to be of creating a peaceful, prosperous, and democratically governed Iraq after Saddam had been overthrown, the invaders were never going to be faced with the sort of humiliating withdrawal that was forced on Eden and the French in 1956. To be accused, as Prime Minister, of having been economical with the truth in the run-up to a war is a great deal more damaging if the war has been lost than if it has been won.

There is, however, one parallel between Suez and Iraq which clearly holds. In both cases, the justification for war in the mind of the Prime Minister went beyond the immediate *casus belli* that was given — recovery of the Suez Canal in the first case and removal of WMD in the second. Eden, on his own testimony, was determined not to appease a dictator who was threatening a vital British interest at a time when the Soviet Union was as menacing as it had ever been. Blair, on his own testimony, was determined not to remain inactive in the face of Islamic terrorism after what had happened in the United States on 11 September 2001, and must be presumed to have shared the unproven American view that Al Qa'ida had high-level links with Iraq. If, therefore, there is a moral as opposed to merely prudential judgement to be made, it will depend, as in all such cases, on whether or not you agree that the end justified the means.[52] Some will say yes, and others no. But it is not something which Lord Hutton, Lord Butler, or any of the contributors to this volume can decide for you.

---

[52] John Kampfner, in his *Blair's Wars* (The Free Press, 2004), p. 265, says of the second dossier, put together on the initiative of Alastair Campbell in the run-up to the Washington summit, 'This was a classic New Labour tactic of the 1990s, playing fast and loose with the facts for what it believed to be a greater good'.

The Hutton Inquiry:
Some Wider Legal Aspects

WILLIAM TWINING

We live in an audit society with a sound-bite culture.[1] In the Hutton Inquiry the Prime Minister, other senior members of the Executive, members of Parliament, BBC journalists and the BBC itself were all called to account in a blaze of publicity; then the auditor himself and his report were subjected to critical scrutiny by the national press. Three sound-bite phrases that were central to Lord Hutton's inquiry were all shown in evidence to be radically ambiguous — 'weapons of mass destruction', 'deployment within 45 minutes', and 'sexed up'. In the second phase more familiar sound-bite expressions were bandied about: 'spin', 'whitewash' and 'cover up'. There is a danger that the whole episode will be remembered largely in such terms.

I was in Britain during the hearings, but I was in the United States when Lord Hutton reported.[2] This underlined the sharp differences in public perceptions of the proceedings and later of the report: Lord Hutton was generally praised for his handling of the inquiry; his analysis of the evidence and nearly all of his specific findings of fact were widely accepted; but several of his most important conclusions were equally widely criticized.

In Britain, like millions of citizens, I followed the proceedings on television, fascinated by the unusually bright light that was shone on the workings of government at a moment of crisis and on a number of shadowy figures who are usually invisible rather than transparent. This was a fascinating and dramatic case study of open government. However, on the same day in January that Lord Hutton reported, a former US Chief Weapons Inspector, David Kaye, told the Senate Armed Services Committee that he no longer believed that Saddam Hussein had significant stocks of illegal

---

[1] I am grateful to Jeffrey Jowell QC, Dawn Oliver and Robert Stevens for some helpful comments.

[2] Lord Hutton, *Report of the Inquiry into the Circumstances Surrounding the Death of Dr David Kelly C.M.G.*, HC 247 (2004) (hereafter Hutton).

weapons or an active programme on the eve of the war. Not surprisingly, David Kaye captured the American headlines and the Hutton Report was relegated to quite succinct summaries on the inside pages. Within days its significance had been reduced to sound-bite references. In the United States, there was hardly any mention of the subsequent controversy in the British press. Within days the report was poorly remembered history.

Largely as a result of David Kaye's testimony, President Bush felt compelled to set up an inquiry into the intelligence about Iraq's weapons of mass destruction. This in turn led a reluctant Prime Minister to set up the Butler Review, which reported on 14 July 2004.[3] That raises questions as to how far Butler has superseded Hutton. So far as the wider issues are concerned, my view is that they complement each other to give a vivid picture of the workings of government.

I have been asked to consider the wider legal implications of the Hutton episode. Jonathan Sumption QC, Counsel for the Government, argued that there is a 'danger of trying to learn general lessons from appalling but wholly exceptional and unpredictable events.'[4] I think that this is broadly true, but that it goes a step too far. In my view, the Hutton episode throws almost no light on the legality, the morality, or the prudence of the war in Iraq — nor should we have expected it to. It only throws indirect light on such matters as the search for 'Weapons of Mass Destruction' or whether the information included in the September dossier was of sufficient strength and reliability to justify military action in Iraq.[5] Nor does it have very much general legal significance in a technical sense.

---

[3] *Review of Intelligence on Weapons of Mass Destruction,* HC 898 (2004) (hereafter Butler).
[4] Quoted in the *Guardian: The Hutton Inquiry and its Impact* (2004), at p. 289.
[5] Hutton p. 2.

Once they have performed a short-term political function, reports of this kind tend to survive mainly as fodder for academic specialists to pick over at leisure. It is still difficult to assess the political impact of the Hutton Report. It exonerated the Prime Minister and others in government from the most serious allegations; it quelled most rumours that doubted that David Kelly had committed suicide; it gave a severe jolt to the BBC at the start to the run-up to the review of its Charter — but opinion is divided on whether it strengthened or weakened its position in the longer term; and it stimulated some further inquiries. I shall suggest that the Hutton episode is of minor significance in relation to political judgments on the war in Iraq, or to the practice of involving judges in public inquiries, or to the law relating to freedom of information and freedom of speech. It is too early to judge whether it will be influential as a model of open government at moments of political crisis; in future some inquiries may be vulnerable to such questions as: why are you being less open than Lord Hutton? Given the unprecedented publication of JIC intelligence material by Lord Butler, we may be seeing the start of a significant trend.[6]

However, the Hutton Report does raise a few issues of a broadly constitutional significance. I shall consider briefly the implications of involving senior judges in politically sensitive inquiries; the terms of reference and how they were interpreted; the procedures adopted; the powers of inquiries; and freedom of information, all of which are intimately related. I shall then touch briefly on the relations between the Executive and the intelligence services, which have now been dealt with more thoroughly in the Butler Report. I shall leave my colleagues to deal with Hutton's

---

[6] However, in respect of the extensive quotations from JIC assessments 'The Government has made it clear that [this] will not be accepted as a precedent for putting these assessments into the public domain in future.' Butler para. 12, p. 3.

implications for journalists and what is perhaps the most important issue — the possible impact of the episode on future relations between the BBC and the government.

The use of judges in quasi-judicial and non-judicial inquiries

Public inquiries are normally set up by Ministers to investigate and pronounce on matters giving rise to serious public concern, such as major disasters, allegations of corruption or of serious impropriety in public life or of police malfeasance. The main objective is to restore public confidence by a formal, independent, and open investigation of the facts, and to make recommendations to prevent a recurrence of the matters causing public concern. Where appropriate this may involve blaming or exonerating individuals, provided that it does not purport to determine legal responsibility. But that is a secondary objective.[7]

The Hutton Inquiry is an example of the peculiarly British practice of using senior judges to conduct quasi-judicial inquiries into politically significant events. Within 24 hours of the news of Dr Kelly's tragic death, a senior judge had undertaken 'Urgently to conduct an investigation into the circumstances surrounding the death of Dr Kelly'. The decision to hold an inquiry, the terms of reference, the decision that it should be chaired by a single senior

---

[7] The recent consultation paper on *Effective Inquiries* is emphatic on the point that the purpose of inquiries is not to determine legal responsibility: 'In summary, the Government believes that a single inquiry should be sufficient to fulfil the aims of establishing facts and preventing recurrence. However, an inquiry should not attempt to establish civil liability, or to deal with allegations of professional misconduct or criminal activity. If needed, other mechanisms must be used to deal with these issues.' *Effective Inquiries: A consultation paper produced by the Department for Constitutional Affairs*, CP 12/04 (May 2004), para. 44, p. 21.

judge, and the choice of the individual judge were all decisions of the Executive — the Prime Minister and his advisers. They were in that sense political decisions made in response to a dramatic and tragic event. The transition from the political to a quasi-judicial process was symbolized by the fact that it was the Lord Chancellor — that most ambiguous of dignitaries — who invited Lord Hutton in for a cup of tea and to undertake the task. Lord Hutton, we are told, accepted immediately. It is not clear whether he could have refused on the ground that this was an inappropriate task for a judge, as several Justices of the US Supreme Court have done in the past.[8] But it is clear that when our Supreme Court is established and the Lord Chancellor (or his successor) will no longer be head of the Judiciary, there will be a sharper demarcation between the Executive and the Judiciary. It may then be easier for individual judges or the Judiciary collectively to refuse such assignments more often.[9] And that will be a good time to reconsider the principles that should govern the involvement of judges in extra-judicial activities. Interestingly, the excellent recent Consultation Paper on *Effective Inquiries* assumes that the practice will continue rather than weighing its costs and benefits.[10]

In this respect the Hutton Inquiry is just the latest in a long succession of instances in which there has been controversy about the appropriateness of employing senior judges to conduct or chair public inquiries in politically sensitive or otherwise controversial areas. It is not a particularly extreme example. This is a complex

---

[8] William H. Rehnquist, *Centennial Crisis* (2004), Epilogue.

[9] The Ministerial Code currently requires ministers to consult the Lord Chancellor about any proposal to appoint a judge to chair a public inquiry. This function will probably be transferred to the Lord Chief Justice. *Effective Inquiries*, para. 28.

[10] Ibid. paras 45–50. At the time of writing, the House of Commons Select Committee on Public Administration is also considering 'Government by Inquiry', but has not yet reported.

subject with a long history. Other countries have used judges in extra-judicial inquiries, but it is probably fair to say that most have tended to be more cautious than the UK in this area.[11] Lords Widgery, Parker, and Diplock were among those who had their fingers burned in respect of Northern Ireland; Scott, Scarman, and Macpherson attracted controversy. Eyebrows have been raised about the Saville Inquiry into Bloody Sunday, which since 1999 has tied up one of our most respected judges, has cost over £150 million pounds, and could lead to a no-win denouement. From the point of view of the individual judge, the invitation to chair an inquiry may often have come to seem like a poisoned chalice.

But is it in the public interest that judges should be given such tasks? The issues are complex, because inquiries are of many different kinds, the extent to which they are divisive varies considerably and so do the procedures. There is a strong body of academic opinion that questions the practice.[12] The more cautious emphasize the importance of the independence of the Judiciary and of maintaining public confidence in judges. They point out that judges by virtue of their training and experience are better equipped to investigate particular past events (what happened?) than to consider future policy (what should happen?); they tend to be better at dealing with precisely defined issues (monocentric inquiries) rather than broad-ranging, diffuse ones (polycentric inquiries).[13] Most agree that judges should as far as possible avoid unnecessarily becoming embroiled in public controversy.

Opposition to the practice has been stronger in the United States, even at moments of extreme national crisis. Nevertheless,

---

[11] Jeffrey Jowell, 'The wrong man for the job', *Guardian*, 3 February 2004.

[12] For example, Robert Stevens, *The English Judges: Their Role in the Changing Constitution* (2002); Jowell, 'The wrong man for the job', n. 11.

[13] Lon Fuller, 'The Forms and Limits of Adjudication', *Harvard Law Review*, 92 (1978), 353.

Supreme Court Justices have undertaken some major extra-judicial assignments at the request of the President: Justice Owen Roberts in respect of Pearl Harbor; Justice Robert Jackson to become chief US Prosecutor at the Nuremberg Trials; and Chief Justice Earl Warren to chair the Commission to inquire into the assassination of President Kennedy. Warren was extremely reluctant to take on the assignment, but had his arm twisted by President Lyndon Johnson; Robert Jackson was keen to take on the Nuremberg Trials, but was heavily criticized by his brethren, who thought that at least he ought to resign. His biographer sums up Chief Justice Stone's attitude as follows:

> For Stone, Justice Jackson's participation in the Nuremberg Trials combined three major sources of irritation: disapproval in principle of non-judicial work, strong objection to the trials on legal and political grounds, the inconvenience and increased burden of work entailed.[14]

The analogy with the United States should not be pressed too far, because the constitutional arrangements are different and part of the concern has been the effect on the workload of the Supreme Court, which has a finite number of Justices. Much of the American concern for a strong and independent 'Third Branch' of government is just because the Federal Courts are called on to decide important, often highly contested issues of state. The more 'political' the role of the Judiciary, the greater is the need for a strong doctrine of separation of powers. It is their independence of the Executive more than their political impartiality that tends to be emphasized in the American debates. Chief Justice Rehnquist, after a careful survey of the history, agrees that the independence and

---

[14] Alpheus T. Mason, *Harlan Fiske Stone: Pillar of the Law* (New York: Viking, 1956), cited by William Rehnquist at p. 240.

reputation of the Judiciary, especially the Supreme Court, is put at risk by involvement of judges in extra-judicial activities, but concludes that at times of national crisis the risks of not using judges when needed may be even greater. Echoing Lincoln's words: 'Shall I save the Constitution, but lose the nation?'

Quis custodiet ipsos custodes? If not judges, who? Who besides a judge or senior lawyer could have designed and presided over an inquisitorial proceeding that involved public examination and cross-examination of witnesses in such an open and revealing manner? I doubt whether an inquiry conducted by a committee drawn from the great and the good (i.e. non-lawyers) or by an elder statesman or a bi-partisan committee of politicians could have revealed nearly so much. The Butler Report contains a unique collection of quotations from JIC assessments, but does not give so much insight as the Hutton Report into the day-to-day operation of government. Its proceedings were arcane — understandably in the circumstances. A quasi-judicial procedure can produce extraordinary detail and openness, but at the almost inevitable cost of narrowing the issues. Judges are needed to operate this kind of proceeding.

The terms of reference

Lord Hutton robustly claimed that he had discretion to interpret his terms of reference. One might say that these were open to three possible interpretations: a narrow one concerned only with the cause of Dr Kelly's death and allocation of blame in connection with it; a broad one dealing with such matters as the accuracy of the information in the September dossier, the justification of the war, and intelligence about weapons of mass destruction; and, thirdly, something in between. Lord Hutton chose the third option.

The narrow issues centre on the question whether Dr Kelly committed suicide or was murdered, and whether anyone should be blamed in any way for any decisions or actions that may have contributed to his death.[15] These issues one might say are recognizably justiciable — i.e. appropriate for adjudication — even though in this case some are concerned with moral rather than legal responsibility. As we know, Lord Hutton dealt with all of these matters, concluding unequivocally that the cause of death was suicide; that the exact motives for suicide were uncertain;[16] that no one should be blamed for contributing to Dr Kelly's death; and that, although the manner of his 'outing' was not improper in the circumstances, more could have been done by the MOD to help and support him.

In theory, Lord Hutton could have stopped there. But clearly that would not have met Government's concerns about the accuracy of Andrew Gilligan's allegations nor public concerns about the way the September dossier was compiled. But if we go beyond a narrow, legalistic interpretation, we get into muddier waters. What issues were to be treated as relevant to the story of Dr Kelly's death? Lord Hutton robustly declared that he was going to focus on five sets of issues.[17] Three are covered by the narrower interpretation; the remaining two are:

(1) issues relating to the preparation of the dossier of 24 September 2002, but not to its accuracy or wording;

---

[15] These narrow issues include: 4a the issue on whether the Government behaved improperly in revealing Dr Kelly's name to the media; 4b whether the Government failed to take proper steps to help and protect Dr Kelly; and 5 the factors which may have led Dr Kelly to take his own life.

[16] 'It is not possible to be certain as to the factors which drove Dr Kelly to commit suicide but ... it is very probable that Professor Hawthorn's opinion ... is correct.' (loss of self-esteem, he withdrew into himself, miscellaneous other pressures). Hutton pp. 306-7.

[17] Hutton pp. 319ff.

(2) issues relating to the BBC's behaviour before and after Andrew Gilligan's allegations impugning the integrity of the Government in preparing the dossier.

Some people had hoped for a broader inquiry into the accuracy of the information in the dossier of 24 September, whether the information included in the dossier was of sufficient strength and reliability to justify military action in Iraq, and even the wider issues of the legality, morality, and wisdom of going to war.[18] Lord Hutton ruled that all of these matters fell outside his terms of reference, mainly on the ground that a broad-ranging inquiry of this kind could not be conducted urgently and much of it was not directly relevant to the circumstances leading up to the death of Dr Kelly. This provoked a storm of criticism from frustrated journalists who had expected more from this highly visible political drama.

In my opinion, Lord Hutton was broadly justified in interpreting the terms of reference in the way he did both for the grounds he gave,[19] but also (1) because the tragic death of an individual is not a good focal point for dealing systematically with such broad and diverse issues, and (2) because these issues have been and will be the subject of other extensive inquiries, both in this country and elsewhere. In preparing this essay I have had to look at eight other recent British reports relating to issues raised by Hutton, to say nothing of reports from the United States, and books such as Hans Blix's memoir.[20] Some of these deal in much

---

[18] My personal view is that the war in Iraq was illegal, immoral, and very imprudent, but these issues also fall outside my terms of reference in this context.

[19] I would dissent on the issue whether the wording of the September dossier was misleading, which was a direct result of Downing Street involvement in the drafting.

[20] Other inquiries: Intelligence and Security Committee: Iraqi Weapons of Mass Destruction — Intelligence and Assessments; House of Commons

more detail than either Lord Hutton or Lord Butler with such matters as the Government's public relations, freedom of information, the BBC's internal procedures, and arrangements for public inquiries.

Indeed, I would go further and say that a lot of criticism would have been avoided if Lord Hutton had also treated the row between Alastair Campbell and the BBC and the BBC's defence of Andrew Gilligan as tangential to the story of the events leading up to David Kelly's death.

Procedure

Lord Hutton displayed his independence by robustly determining the procedure to be followed and maintaining firm control of the proceedings. At present there is no statutory framework for public inquiries and the Chairman has a wide discretion to determine and control the procedure. Building on the experience of prior inquiries, especially the Scott Inquiry into Arms for Iraq and the Macpherson Inquiry into the murder of Stephen Lawrence, Lord Hutton adopted a quasi-judicial procedure which is a Benthamic

---

Foreign Affairs Select Committee: Report into the Use of Intelligence in the Buildup to the Iraq War; Report on Andrew Gilligan's Evidence (corroborating finding that AG's more serious allegations were unfounded); Independent Review of Government Communications (Phillis) Interim Report, August 2003; Final Report, January 2004; Consultation Paper on Effective Inquiries (Dept. Constitutional Affairs CP 12/04, May 2004). Subsequently, Lord Butler's Review of Intelligence on Weapons of Mass Destruction, HC 898, July 2004; BBC Review (Neil Report, June 2004); Report on Foreign Policy Aspects of the War Against Terrorism; Iraq Survey Group (USA); Evidence to US Congressional Committees; Hans Blix, *Disarming Iraq* (2004), etc.

mixture of civil and common law approaches with the following characteristics.[21]

(1) It was 'inquisitorial' in that the Chairman rather than any interested parties controlled who was called as a witness, what documents were produced, and, to a large extent, what questions were asked.

(2) It resembled common law proceedings in emphasizing oral testimony and the examination and cross-examination of witnesses in public.[22]

(3) The style was investigative rather than contentious or disputatious: in the first stage witnesses were examined by counsel for the inquiry 'in a neutral way';[23] in the second stage, some witnesses whose conduct might be the subject of criticism in the report were recalled (or called for the first time) to be examined further by counsel for the inquiry, their own counsel, and counsel for other parties — all subject to permission of the Chairman.

(4) The most striking innovation was the creation of a website on which almost all of the evidence was posted immediately, so that although the proceedings were not televised, the media and the public at large had access to almost all of the information presented to the inquiry. This meant that in theory at least everyone could make up their own minds on the basis of almost the same evidence as Lord Hutton. The report organized and analysed the evidence, made findings of fact based on that evidence, and allocated responsibility by exonerating or blaming

---

[21] Jeremy Bentham generally favoured an inquisitorial approach, but he argued that emphasis on publicity and cross-examination combined to making the English system of procedure 'perhaps the least bad extant, instead of being among the worst.' *Rationale of Judicial Evidence*, ed. J. S. Mill (1827), vol. 1, p. 585.

[22] Ibid.

[23] Hutton para. 4, p. 1.

individual actors in connection with the events treated by Lord Hutton as relevant.

I have four comments on the procedure adopted.

(1) This kind of investigative procedure is well-suited to open and thorough determination of the facts about particular past events. However, whatever procedure is adopted, criticism and exoneration of individuals is a tricky matter, because an inquiry is not meant to determine legal responsibility, but there are almost no settled criteria for determining moral or political responsibility in this kind of situation. Nor are there settled standards of proof. Furthermore, it requires due process, which can be time-consuming.[24]

'Naming and blaming' produces sound-bites in ways that detailed analysis often does not. The main criticisms in the media of both Hutton and Butler have centred on their refusal to name and blame individuals in government. Is this reluctance due to pro-establishment bias? Or is it due to concerns about fairness to the individuals concerned?[25] Is it due to a concern not to pre-empt issues that may be the subject of legal proceedings?[26] Is it because of a lack of clear criteria for making such judgments? Or is it that decisions whether ministers or public servants should keep their jobs are really not the job of public inquiries? This is a grey area that needs clarification. What the Hutton and Butler inquiries have shown is that there is a wide gap between the expectations of the media and the public, on the one hand, and those who conduct *ad hoc* public inquiries on the other.

---

[24] The 'Salmon principles' provide safeguards for any person who is likely to be the subject of criticism in a public inquiry as a witness or interested party. The six Salmon principles were set out in the report of the Royal Commission on Tribunals of Inquiry under the chairmanship of Lord Justice Salmon (1966).

[25] See the Salmon principles above.

[26] See above n. 7.

(2) The kind of investigative procedure adopted by Lord Hutton is well-suited to open and thorough determination of the facts about particular past events; it may not be so well-suited to recommending changes in general policy or procedures for the future — in this case the behaviour of the Downing Street Press Office, the JIC, and the BBC's internal procedures — because this kind of issue often requires a broader focus and expertise on matters on which judges may be no more qualified to make judgments than well-informed citizens. As with similar inquiries, Lord Hutton's analysis of the evidence and his specific findings of fact (e.g. on the cause of Dr Kelly's death, the accuracy of Andrew Gilligan's allegations) have been subject to much less controversy than his judgments on blameworthiness and his general criticism of the BBC's editorial and management systems (Chapter 8).

(3) There is a puzzle about why the Hutton Inquiry was so much more of a media event than any other Iraq-related inquiry before that. I would suggest that it has a lot to do with the procedure adopted. This preserved those features that make the common law more telegenic than the civil law — orality, questioning of witnesses, publicity. Despite the exclusion of TV cameras, this helped to make the Hutton Inquiry exceptionally newsworthy: a courtroom drama provided a focus for a human tragedy connected to high politics and great political issues. It is also striking that Lord Hutton obtained much more co-operation and adduced more detail than the two Parliamentary select committees that had previously reported.

(4) Lord Hutton sat alone. It has been suggested that if he had sat with assessors who were, for example, experts on intelligence and the BBC, he might have been able to make better-informed judgments. That is possible. But in a centrifugal case such as this, what kind of expertise would be most useful? The procedure adopted was not appropriate for evaluating the reliability of intelligence; an assessor might have advised differently about JIC-

Executive interface, but was not expertise also needed into the causes of Dr Kelly's death or the Downing Street Press Office or how Dr Kelly was treated by the Ministry of Defence? The use of assessors might also have slowed down proceedings.

Inquiry powers and freedom of information

As this was a non-statutory inquiry Lord Hutton had no powers to subpoena witnesses or to compel the production of documents. This did not impede this inquiry because the Prime Minister had ordered, and Lord Hutton secured, full co-operation of nearly all the relevant people. If anyone had refused to comply the main sanctions would have been informal, notably adverse publicity. If the inquiry had been set up under the Tribunals of Inquiry (Evidence) Act, 1921, powers to compel the attendance of witnesses and the production of documents would have been backed by the possible threat of proceedings for contempt of court. Experience suggests that the effectiveness of tribunals is likely to be enhanced if they have such powers, even if in practice they are kept in reserve as a last resort. However, proceedings for contempt are portentous, formal, and likely to be slow. In the consultation paper on *Effective Inquiries* it is proposed that such powers should be part of a general statutory framework, but that failure to attend as a witness or to produce documents or to take an oath or affirmation, if required, should be made a summary offence, subject to lesser sanctions.[27] This is already provided for under some subject-specific legislation, such as the NHS Act,[28] and is reported to work quite well. It is recommended that there should

---

[27] *Effective Inquiries*, paras 58–74.
[28] Section 84 of the National Health Service Act, 1977.

also be sanctions, short of contempt, for destroying or distorting evidence.[29] These recommendations seem sensible. Fortunately, none of these issues arose during the Hutton Inquiry.

A distinction needs to be drawn between presenting evidence to an inquiry and making that evidence public. Some commentators have suggested that the procedure adopted has important implications for the law relating to freedom of information. That is misleading. The Freedom of Information Act is not yet in force; a great deal of the evidence adduced and displayed would almost certainly have been exempted under the Act.[30] The documents which so graphically revealed the day-to-day workings of government in crisis — emails, minutes, jottings, and Alastair Campbell's diary — would almost all have been exempted. If the Act had been in force, they would have been revealed in spite of not because of it. Information was adduced because officials were instructed to give full co-operation; it was publicly displayed because Lord Hutton appears to have proceeded on a presumption of full disclosure; only a few documents marked 'secret' or 'top secret' were withheld and a few other items specifically requested by the Cabinet Office or other departments.

It seems very unlikely that the Hutton Report will lead directly to any amendments to the Freedom of Information Act; it may or it may not fortify the recommendation of the Phillis Report

---

[29] Ibid. paras 73–74. Some potentially complex issues about public interest immunity, privileges of witnesses, and confidentiality will also need to be resolved in a flexible manner that takes account of the diversity of inquiries. Until now, many of the issues relating to rules of evidence in inquiries have been more extensively debated in Australia and Canada than in England and Wales.

[30] Also, an inquiry is not a public authority so is not itself covered by the Freedom of Information Act. The Act will come into force in January 2005.

(the Government Communications Review Group)[31] that officials should interpret the Act liberally. It is too early to judge whether it will be influential as a model of open government at moments of political crisis; it is possible that some future inquiries may be vulnerable to such questions as: why are you being less open than Lord Hutton was? So the Hutton episode may affect the culture of secrecy, but not the law on freedom of information.

The relations between government and the intelligence services

The chapter on the compilation of the two main dossiers is for me the most interesting in the report. Lord Hutton reconstructs the story in fascinating detail and convincingly shows that the allegation that the Government knowingly included false information in the dossier was unfounded. But it also revealed the extent of the involvement of the Downing Street Press Office in what was presented as an intelligence report.

The Butler Review has explored in detail issues relating to relations between the JIC and the Executive. It has concluded that the September dossier was misleading especially in regard to the reliability of its sources and to the '45 minute' claim. Although the Report is rather gentle on individuals, including Alastair Campbell and the then Chairman of the JIC, it recommends unequivocally that in future a clear line should be drawn between advocacy documents and intelligence assessments. Intelligence assessments should be 'owned' by the intelligence community; advocacy documents should be 'owned' by the politicians. In these respects the Butler Report has superseded the Hutton Report and I am in general agreement with these judgments.

---

[31] See above n. 20.

Here I confine myself to two brief comments. First, immediately the September dossier was published it was clear that the document was at the very least ambiguous in implying that the 45-minute weapons were 'Weapons of Mass Destruction' and in failing to distinguish between battlefield weapons and long-range weapons.[32] When the press misinterpreted the document in a way that sensationalized the ambiguities, no attempt was made by anyone in Government to rectify the seriously misleading impression that had been created. The main actors who were publicly revealed to have been involved in preparing the document washed their hands of responsibility for its interpretation.[33] Yet quite stringent requirements of retraction were demanded of the BBC.

Second, unlike in the United States, the intelligence services have not been made the main scapegoat for things that went wrong. There are suggestions, not yet pronounced on, that the CIA was subject to direct and prolonged political pressure in respect of

---

[32] The Butler Report also emphasizes the dropping of caveats about the reliability of the intelligence. The Intelligence and Security Committee also pointed out in relation to the September dossier: 'The first draft of the Prime Minister's foreword contained the following sentence: "*The case I make is not that Saddam could launch a nuclear attack on London or another part of the UK (he could not).*" ... It was unfortunate that this point was removed from the published version of the foreword and not highlighted elsewhere.' Intelligence and Security Committee (see above n. 20), para. 83. Dr Brian Jones in evidence to the Hutton Inquiry pointed out that the term 'Weapons of Mass Destruction' refers to nuclear weapons and some, but not all, chemical and biological weapons. At some points the '45 minute' claim was confined to 'some chemical and biological weapons', but at others the term 'weapons of mass destruction' was used in relation to the claim, including the Prime Minister's Foreword.

[33] See evidence of Mr Hoon at pp. 149–50 denying any duty to correct false impressions created by the press on the ground that they do not like to correct stories. In similar vein, John Scarlett at p. 151; Alastair Campbell, evidence, 19 August: 'I do not write headlines for the Evening Standard'.

their assessments on Iraq. It seems that this may be less of a problem in this country and that 'the strain' experienced by the JIC in respect of the September dossier was a unique aberration.[34]

It might be argued that the intelligence community is inescapably involved in a political process. In this view, it is practically impossible to maintain a sharp line between fact and value in making intelligence assessments; intelligence analysts will very often have a clear idea of what their political masters want to hear; they can be steered towards particular conclusions without overt pressure; and they may be influenced by the desire to please. In short, the idea of an independent, impartial intelligence service is a pipe-dream.

I disagree. As with judicial independence, the dangers of pressure and bias are there, but it is of the essence of professionalism consciously to discount such biases and to make judgments without regard to what one's clients or patients or sponsors want to hear. One of the encouraging aspects of what was revealed by the Hutton Inquiry was the professionalism exhibited by members of the intelligence community, including Dr Jones and Dr Kelly himself. They, it seems, had a clear idea of the difference between intelligence reports and political advocacy. But a question remains whether extra buffers are needed to ensure that political influence on intelligence analysis and assessment is minimized.

---

[34] The Butler Report makes it clear that the JIC claiming 'ownership' of the September dossier was unprecedented and was a mistake that should never be repeated.

Conclusion

To sum up: The Hutton episode is not of great legal significance. Although it was criticized, the Hutton Report was not an extreme example of the danger of involving judges in political controversy. Issues of freedom of speech and the repercussions of the report for the BBC will be dealt with by my colleagues. Lurking in the interstices of this substantial and diffuse report are some issues about inquests, the law of defamation as it affects journalists, and so on. It raises a few constitutional issues that I have touched on. It is a wonderful study in open government, but I suggest that this is less to do with the law relating to freedom of information than to the culture of secrecy that has now been more extensively canvassed by the Phillis Report. Public inquiries play an important role in our public life. They are most useful in clarifying issues and determining facts, but we should not expect too much of them in respect of attributing political, professional, or legal responsibility.

Discussion

MICHAEL BELOFF

I want to add a few footnotes to William Twining's essay, and then turn to a subject which he has by design omitted, but which for many lawyers has been the most interesting and controversial aspect of Lord Hutton's findings — whether his criticisms of the BBC give sufficient weight to their right of freedom of expression guaranteed under the European Convention on Human Rights and the domestic Human Rights Act 1998.

The first point is this. There was no legal obligation upon the Government to set up the Hutton Inquiry at all. It was a purely political decision. Dr David Kelly's suicide would, in ordinary circumstances, have been dealt with by Coroner's inquest; and the recent decision of the House of Lords, adjusting the domestic legislation to Convention imperatives, would have allowed for a sufficiently deep investigation into the underlying causes of his suicide, as long as it did not identify any individual allegedly responsible nor address any issue of civil or criminal liability.[34] As it was, the actual Coroner who enjoyed jurisdiction felt, in the hallowed phrase of the third judge in a three-judge appellate court, that he add nothing to add.[35]

---

[34] *R (Middleton) v West Somerset Coroner*, 2004 2 WLR 800.
[35] John Bingham and Stuart Coles, 'Coroner rules against fresh Kelly hearing', *Independent*, 16 March 2004. See Coroners' Act 1988 Section 17A for the legal basis for the Coroner's decision.

The second point is that the 'big issue', the legality of the invasion of the sovereign state of Iraq, did not fall within Lord Hutton's remit and could not usefully have done so. It has excited much debate among public international lawyers. The case against has been powerfully articulated by, amongst others, Lord Alexander QC in his Tom Sargant Memorial Lecture;[36] and concerns within the Foreign and Commonwealth Office were illustrated by the resignation of Elizabeth Wilmshurst,[37] a senior legal adviser. The Attorney General's supportive advice has only been recently published in summary form,[38] and to that extent, the case in favour has not been so fully deployed or at any rate publicized.

Who was right on that issue could be tested at any rate in theory at the International Court of Justice in The Hague — although there was an audacious but unavailing attempt by the Campaign for Nuclear Disarmament to obtain a judicial review in the High Court of the Government's decision to invade without a second UN resolution.[39] Yet the pronouncements of an eminent lawyer such as Lord Hutton *outside* the appropriate legal forum would command respect, but would not be legally binding. Any trial of the Prime Minister's decision that United Kingdom troops should join the invasion will take place before the bar of history.

The third point is that the contrast between the public view of the inquiry process and the inquiry outcome was preordained. On the one hand, there was universal admiration for the manner in which Lord Hutton handled the inquiry. He combined efficiency and expedition, and mindful of the need to be fair to all parties — since his criticism, although lacking the force of an order of Court,

---

[36] Justice press release, 10 October 2003.
[37] BBC News, 27 February 2004.
[38] BBC News, 17 March 2003.
[39] 2004 ACD 85.

could have severe consequences for its objects[40] — did not sacrifice justice to convenience. This was no mean feat, since it is a feature of the majority of inquiries that, like Topsy, they just grow. As a participant advocate in three, the Crown Agents Inquiry,[41] the Scarman Inquiry into the Brixton Riots in 1981,[42] and an inquiry into a marine collision in Singapore,[43] I am well aware of how time estimates for duration conventionally fall widely short of the mark. On the other hand, Lord Hutton's substantive conclusions commanded less than universal applause. The explanation is obvious. The issues assigned to his consideration were more political than legal and were ones on which judgments were generally formed before his inquiry and consequently unchanged by it.

Although Lord Hutton's exercise was in form an inquiry, it rapidly took on — at least in the perception of those who reported it — an adversarial contest with the Government on one side and the BBC on the other. Few, if any, who participated in or followed it were other than surprised by Lord Hutton's acquittal of the Government and criticism of the BBC: most expected him to find fault on both sides.[44] And there was certainly room for different opinions on the primary facts which he (and subsequently Lord Butler) painstakingly analysed: for example, the question remains as to why it was that the intelligence dossier upon which the Government relied to justify the invasion underwent changes between its original text and the final published version, although

---

[40] See *Three Rivers DC v Bank of England*, 2004 3 All ER 168, at p. 181 d–e.

[41] *Report of the Tribunal appointed to inquire into certain issues arising out of the operation of the Crown Agents' finances in the years 1962–71*, HC 264 (HMSO, 1982)

[42] *Report into the Brixton Disorder: 10–12 April 1981*, Cmnd 8427 (HMSO, 1982).

[43] *Report of the Commission of Inquiry into the Collision of the Drillship Eniwetok with the Sentosa Cableway on 29 January 1983* (30 December 1983).

[44] Private information from participant QC.

the underlying intelligence information had not changed at all. That might suggest to some either an overbearing Government or an over-pliant intelligence service;[45] Lord Hutton's view was that, if the latter were prepared to accept the former's suggestions as to alterations, then all remained for the best in the best of all possible worlds. Subconscious influence was the limit of his critique. Lord Butler for his part merely referred to 'a weakness on the part of all those who were involved in putting together the dossier',[46] giving birth to a novel legal principle that if everyone is guilty, no one is.[47] But the debate has clearly not reached closure among politicians, press or public. *Tot homines, quot sententiae*.[48] We would both hope and expect by contrast more commonality of opinion from judges sitting in courts of law.

My fourth point is that, had Lord Hutton continued to serve as a Lord of Appeal in Ordinary after submission of his report, instead of retiring, he might have risked losing, in the eyes of some, that appearance of being above the fray, which is essential to public confidence in the independence and impartiality of the judiciary. I add at once that he was in no sense the author of his own misfortune as was, arguably but accidentally, Lord Hoffmann whose amnesia about his links with Amnesty, an interested party in the *Pinochet* litigation, caused the nullification of the first judgment and the reconvening of a fresh House of Lords' appellate committee to determine whether the General could be extradited

---

[45] See Lord Owen, 'How to read the Butler Report: start with the vital annexe', *The Times*, 17 July 2004.

[46] Lord Butler replying to a question at the launch of the Butler Report on 14 July 2004.

[47] A maxim flatteringly adapted by Sir Simon Jenkins in an op. ed. piece in *The Times*, 21 July 2004.

[48] This Latin phrase is now, of course, banished from the vocabulary of the Courts.

to Spain.[49] My conclusion, contrary to William Twining's, is that judges ought not to be asked to undertake tasks that are properly those of our elected representatives. They are chosen for those tasks because of the respect in which they are held: but that respect may be damaged by the very performance of those tasks, especially in an era when whether *proprio motu* or *force majeure* they are, in the context of their intra-curricular activities, drawn through judicial review into decisions with a political impact, albeit not in point of form political decisions.[50] It is, indeed, part of the ethics of the judiciary in the United States of America that they should abstain from so doing: the American Canons of Judicial Conduct provide 'A judge should not accept appointment to a government committee or other position that is concerned with issues of fact or policy or matters other than the improvement of the law, the legal system or the administration of justice'. The Warren Commission, dealing with a unique occasion in the 20th century of the assassination of a serving President, was a rare exception which illuminated the rule.[51] If it is felt that legal skills are required in connection with the conduct of such inquiry, then, for the future, consideration might be given to use of senior Queens Counsel without ambition for judicial wigs or robes — another reason why that rank should be preserved.[52]

I now turn to the separate question of law. Part of the criticism by Lord Hutton of the BBC is premised on his analysis of the right to freedom of expression, as defined in Article 10 of the European

---

[49] 2000 1 AC 199.

[50] See Michael Beloff QC, 'Judicial review in England and Wales — "the state of the art"', *Jersey Law Review*, 7 (1) (February 2003), 29.

[51] See the essay on 'Judicial ethics' by Lord Bingham of Cornhill in *The Business of Judging* (Oxford University Press, 2000), at p. 76.

[52] This is not a job application!

Convention on Human Rights.[53] In paragraph 280 of his report he said

> Counsel for the BBC and for Mr Gilligan were right to state that communication by the media of information (including information obtained by reporters) on matters of public interest and importance is a vital part of life in a democratic society. However the right to communicate such information is subject to the qualification (which itself exists for the benefit of a democratic society) that false accusations of fact impugning the integrity of others, including politicians, should not be made by the media. Where a reporter is intending to broadcast or publish information impugning the integrity of others the management of his broadcasting company or newspaper should ensure that a system is in place whereby his editor or editors give careful consideration to the wording of the report and to whether it is right in all the circumstances to broadcast or publish it.[54]

In so concluding Lord Hutton referred to the important judgment in the case of *Reynolds v Times Newspapers Ltd*[55] (*Reynolds*). In *New York Times v Sullivan*[56] (*Sullivan*), the US Supreme Court, relying on the first amendment to the United States' Constitution,[57] created a 'public figure' defence which all but extinguished the prospect of success, malice apart, in defamation actions where the plaintiff had that status. The European Convention is more nuanced;[58] so it is

---

[53] Now domesticated by the Human Rights Act 1998 ('HRA').

[54] Hutton para. 280, pp. 193–4.

[55] 2001 2 AC 127.

[56] 1964 376 US 254.

[57] 'Congress shall make no law abridging freedom of speech or of the Press.'

[58] Article 10 (2) states that 'The exercise of these freedoms, since it carries with it duties and responsibilities, may be subject to such formalities, conditions, restrictions or penalties as are prescribed by law and are necessary in a democratic society for the protection of the reputation or rights of others.'

unsurprising that our Supreme Court (as it already is in all but name) declined in *Reynolds* to follow its American counterpart in *Sullivan*. It did, however, broaden the terms of the defence of qualified privilege in libel (which protects against actions for even inaccurate and damaging statements of fact where there is considered to be a duty to impart and a correlative interest to receive) by extending it to the media reporting on issues of compelling political interest. As a *quid pro quo* they insisted on press responsibility, for which Lord Nicholls, who gave the leading speech, proposed a non-exhaustive 10 element test. [59]

On one view Mr Gilligan comprehensively failed the tests because the suggestion that the Government probably knew that the '45 minute' claim in the dossier was dodgy was not supported even by his source, Dr David Kelly. Equally Mr Gilligan did not obey the primary rule of natural justice, embedded in the 7th of Lord Nicholls' elements, that is to say to put the charge to the persons accused in advance of publication.

The Hutton approach has provoked controversy among media lawyers. Jonathan Coad[60] considers it was correct, Professor Conor Gearty[61] that it was not. For my part, if pure Nicholls is refined into pure Hutton, the media well may be deterred from their proper pursuits. It is impossible to see how, in the real world, the BBC (or equivalent media organization) would be in a position to check all its output all the time for potentially 'false accusations of fact impugning the integrity of others including politicians' and decline to broadcast anything that might pose such a risk. The full

---

[59] *Reynolds*, at pp. 204–5.
[60] *Entertainment Law Review* (2004), p. 157.
[61] *Guardian*, 24 February 2004.

implications of the *Reynolds* judgment are yet to be worked out,[62] but on any view, it does license in the public interest the occasional dissemination of information that is not accurate. As Lord Nicholls said

> The press discharges vital functions as a bloodhound as well as a watchdog. The court should be slow to conclude that a publication was not in the public interest, and therefore the public had no right to know especially when the information is in the field of political discussion.[63]

In any event English defamation law has always distinguished between pre-emptive and responsive action. Injunctions are not granted if the defendant indicates an intention to raise a defence whether it be of justification, fair comment, or qualified privilege.[64] The party allegedly defamed is left to his remedy in damages. A media with pretensions to a role as a Fourth Estate should, although not recklessly, have the courage of its reporters' convictions: publish and be sued, for it ain't over till the jury foreman returns.

What would a jury have made of the Gilligan allegation that the September dossier was 'sexed up', seen in its full context, especially if they had heard witnesses on either side being cross-examined? Would they have thought that the sting of the offending broadcast lay (narrowly) in the proposition that the Government deliberately published inaccurate intelligence, or (broadly) that the Government coloured intelligence they thought to be true: and if the latter, would they have found the broadcast

---

[62] See F. A. Trindle, 'Defamatory statements and political discussion', *Law Quarterly Review*, 116 (2000), 185; K. Williams, 'Defaming politicians: the not so common law', *Modern Law Review*, 63 (2000), 748.

[63] *Reynolds*, at p. 205.

[64] *Gatley on Libel and Slander*, 10th edn, para. 25.1.

defensible? It is, of course, impossible to know. What is clear is that Lords Hutton and Butler, by acquitting the Government of wilful deception (where the standard of proof is properly very high[65]), left unanswered the question of how culpable (if culpable at all) the Government were in publishing intelligence which was — it now appears — not the whole truth. Neither the Prime Minister nor even Alastair Campbell can claim to be above the law; but equally libel law allows them opportunity for redress in a public forum, of which neither will, of course, avail himself.

More orthodox is the second conclusion reached by Lord Hutton concerning the legal framework in which the media operate.

> I am unable to accept, in the context of Mr Gilligan's broadcasts, the distinction which he and the BBC rely on between a report that the BBC believed that the Government probably knew that the 45 minutes claim was wrong and a report that a source had told the BBC that the Government probably knew that the 45 minutes claim was wrong. This is not a distinction recognised by the law in relation to actions for defamation.[66]

This is indisputably right. A law which allowed persons to disseminate untruths simply on the basis that they have been told them by someone else, would protect not virtuous whistleblowers, but vicious scandalmongers. Such an argument is the last refuge of a forensic failure. But the BBC had better points; and even if Lord Hutton did not accept them, he has not had, unlike when he sat as a Lord of Appeal in Ordinary, the very last word.

---

[65] *Khawaja and Khera v Secretary of State for the Home Department*, 1984 AC 74, per Lord Scarman at p. 112.
[66] Hutton, para. 282, p. 194.

And that, in respect of both the Hutton and Butler reports, is as it should be. Whether or not persons selected to chair such inquiries, be they senior judges or senior civil servants or others from the ranks of the great and the good, should take it on themselves to hold individual politicians personally responsible for their errors is beside the point, for they have no legal or constitutional role to prosecute or convict. If politicians have committed serious mistakes, it is for their party, Parliament, and, ultimately the public to pronounce the verdict, making use as they think fit of the facts comprehensively assembled and any opinions cogently pronounced in such reports.[67] If for whatever reason all decline to say 'guilty', that, in a democracy, is their right.

---

[67] A YouGov poll commissioned by the *Sunday Times* after publication of the Butler Report (fieldwork 16–17 July 2004), recorded that 56% of the public believed that the Prime Minister made the decision to go to war in Iraq regardless of the intelligence. Nonetheless it also suggested that he would lead the Labour Party to victory at the next General Election.

The Lightning Flash on
the Road to Baghdad:
Issues of Evidence

PETER HENNESSY

It was Oliver Franks who likened the Suez affair to 'a flash of lightning on a dark night', illuminating a landscape long in the making but not fully appreciated until the limits of British power were cruelly exposed when the UK went to war with France and Israel against Egypt in 1956.[1] Franks himself was quite an illuminator when he led *his* team of privy counsellors in its inquiry into the origins of the Falklands War in 1982.[2] But his report fell far short, in terms of light shed on the processes of government, when one compares it to the combined beams of Lords Hutton[3] and Butler.[4]

From the Prime Minister's Office and the Cabinet Room to the cells inside the Secret Intelligence Service (SIS) building where the incoming agents' reports are tested and validated; from the real-time dealings of No. 10 Downing Street and the media and the way some journalists operate *sub rosa* with private Whitehall contacts to the Wednesday-afternoon tweakings of the Joint Intelligence Committee (JIC) — 'the highest drafting committee in the land', as one of its members described it recently[5] — the Hutton hearings' transcripts and the Butler report are *sans pareil*. Taken together, they represent a lightning flash of a kind that no historians of government or historians of intelligence have seen before in the UK.

---

[1] Peter Hennessy and Caroline Anstey, *Moneybags and Brains: The Anglo-American 'Special Relationship' since 1945*, Strathclyde/*Analysis* Paper, No.1, (Department of Government, University of Strathclyde, 1990), p. 10.

[2] *Falkland Islands Review. Report of a Committee of Privy Counsellors*, Cmnd 8787, (HMSO, 1983).

[3] Lord Hutton, *Report of the Inquiry into the Circumstances Surrounding the Death of Dr David Kelly C.M.G.*, HC 247 (Stationery Office, 28 January 2004) (hereafter Hutton).

[4] *Review of Intelligence on Weapons of Mass Destruction. Report of a Committee of Privy Counsellors*, HC 898 (Stationery Office, 14 July 2004) (hereafter Butler).

[5] Private information.

If, somehow, Kipling were with us to read and sift the two reports, he would describe them — as he did the impact of the Boer War on the British Empire — as 'no end of a lesson'[6] for everyone involved at all levels from the Prime Minister down. And these reports were not the results of any voluntary exercise in openness on the part of the Blair Government. Just think what it took to stimulate those crackles of electricity which produced the lightning flash — two unforeseen events: the suicide of a weapons expert in July 2003; and President George W. Bush's decision in January 2004 to commission an inquiry into Iraq-related intelligence on weapons of mass destruction.

The two British reports which resulted dovetail quite well. Lord Hutton worked as judges do by assessing the evidence in terms of charges made, leading to 'acquittals', 'convictions', and, in one case a 'non-proven' (in the sense that he thought the Chairman of the JIC, John Scarlett, may have been 'subconsciously influenced'[7] by the Prime Minister's press and presentation people in No. 10 making suggestions on the wording and shaping of the September 2002 dossier on Iraq's weapons of mass destruction[8]). Robin Butler and his colleagues worked more like contemporary historians reconstructing reality as best they could from documents and oral evidence, recreating mood and context — if not motivation — as they went.

As any historian of intelligence knows, it is a peculiarly vexing sub-branch of the craft especially in the United Kingdom with its rich fictional literature supplemented by a fuzzy but quite powerful collective memory which tends to believe, thanks to the 'Ultra' story and the signals intelligence (SIGINT) triumphs of the

---

[6] Rudyard Kipling, *The Complete Verse* (Kyle Cathie, 1996), pp. 242–3. The poem in which the line is embedded is called 'The Lesson' (1899–1902).
[7] Hutton p. 320.
[8] *Iraq's Weapons of Mass Destruction: The Assessment of the British Government* (Stationery Office, 24 September 2002).

Second World War which have emerged, bit by bit, over the past 30 years, that unless the UK and its intelligence allies have every tyrant wired for sound 24 hours a day, the resulting surprise when such figures do something nasty and unexpected amounts to an 'intelligence failure'. Media news rooms are particularly prone to this delusion which, among several other distortions, exaggerates hugely the penetration and/or duration of British crypanalytical successes against the Germans. A former Chief of the Secret Intelligence Service could wax almost lyrical on the benefits and costs of this image, including the myths of relative ubiquity and omniscience that often surround his old agency thanks to the books and films, especially the Bond ones. (It has been estimated 'that half the world's population has seen a Bond film.'[9]) Largely because of the myth associated with British intelligence, the retired 'C' put it, 'When we make the final approach and ask someone to help the British as an agent, as often as not they almost stand to attention.' But, he went on, our reach is exaggerated. 'All we can do is provide cats-eyes in the dark' on a very difficult road through dangerous countryside.[10]

Historians, like their fellow hunter-gatherers in the intelligence world, have to draw out from imperfect and incomplete strands what Fernand Braudel called 'that thin wisp of tomorrow which can be guessed at and very nearly grasped'.[11] Did we succeed to any degree in anticipating that mixture of problems, processes, and human fallibilities which produced the difficulties which Butler and Hutton between them had to judge? Up to a point we did.

---

[9] Jeremy Black, *The Politics of James Bond: From Fleming's Novels to the Big Screen* (Praeger, 2001), p. xiii.

[10] Private information.

[11] Fernand Braudel, *A History of Civilisations* (Penguin edn, 1993), p. xxxviii.

For example, a Ditchley Foundation Conference on 'The Future of Intelligence in Democracies' held in October 1997, at which both breeds of hunter-gatherer were well represented (including some British officials whose input was later central to both inquiries), produced a list of five 'consensual givens' of relevance to the Iraq problem as it manifested itself in the longer run-up to war (three and five could have been written with Saddam and 9/11 respectively in mind):

> 1: That special intelligence capabilities would be necessary to reduce the number of secrets possessed by potential threateners of national security.
> 2: That the acquisition of such 'secrets' would diminish thereby the opacity and danger of the 'mysteries' that would remain.
> 3: That the value-added material which only secret sources and methods could provide would enable customers to check the public positions of potential adversaries against reality and to calibrate more effectively the indications of risk and menace which could be gleaned from open sources.
> 4: That certain aspects of 'peacekeeping', not least the maintenance of the nuclear taboo that had held since August 1945, depended to a large degree on secret capacities.
> 5: That successful counter-terrorism depended upon top-flight intelligence frequently pooled with other members of a constellation of intelligence 'clubs'.[12]

A little later, this was converted into a menu depicting how these 'givens' might appear in a list of British intelligence priorities in the late 1990s, the first two of which read:

---

[12] Peter Hennessy, 'The Future of Intelligence in Democracies: Scope, Justification and Control', Ditchley Conference Report No. D97/12 (Ditchley Foundation, 1997), p. 1.

- Weapons-of-mass-destruction (WMD). There are sufficient states with sufficient reach to bring nuclear, chemical or biological destruction to the UK home base for this to be of primary concern for the foreseeable future.

- Terrorism
(a) State-sponsored (which could be linked to WMD capabilities).
(b) Non-state-sponsored e.g. Middle Eastern or North African Groups ...[13]

The Ditchley conference, including the past and present CIA officers in attendance, discussed the most important human requirement of senior intelligence figures when dealing with their ministerial customers — that of keeping them illusion-free.

This has never been better put than by Sir Maurice Oldfield when, as 'C' in March 1974, he was summoned by the new Foreign Secretary, Jim Callaghan, who asked him what his job was for. 'My job, Secretary of State,' Oldfield replied, 'is to bring you unwelcome news.'[14] (A story, incidentally, which Tony Blair said he 'liked' when the Father of the House of Commons, Tam Dalyell, drew it to his attention in the summer of 2003).[15] The Oldfield criterion was quoted at the Ditchley conference and it was subscribed to personally by two intelligence figures (who were not at Ditchley) upon whom the Butler spotlight fell most intensely, Sir

---

[13] Peter Hennessy, 'The Itch After the Amputation? The Purposes of British Intelligence as the Century Turns: An Historical Perspective and a Forward Look', in K. G. Robertson (ed.), *War, Resistance and Intelligence: Essays in Honour of M. R. D. Foot* (Leo Cooper/Pen and Sword, 1999), p. 236.

[14] Ibid. p. 239.

[15] House of Commons, *Official Report*, 3 July 2003, col. 601; Tam Dalyell to Tony Blair, 5 July 2003; Tony Blair to Tam Dalyell, 16 July 2003. I am grateful to Mr Dalyell for sending me copies of this correspondence.

Richard Dearlove when Chief of SIS, and John Scarlett, when Chairman of the Joint Intelligence Committee, the JIC.[16]

Around the time Dearlove was appointed 'C' in 1999, a Braudelian 'thin wisp' of tomorrow and a hint of the problem to come when JIC material became used for political advocacy as well as intelligence analysis with the publication of the Government's September 2002 dossier on *Iraq's Weapons of Mass Destruction* (a fusion of purposes strongly criticised by Butler[17]) was *just* discernible to the intelligence historian. For example, in my study of *The Prime Minister: The Office and Its Holders since 1945*, published by Penguin Press in September 2000, I was able to write that at

> the end of 1999 there were signs that Mr Blair was toying with the idea of ending the traditional (and much-prized) distinction between intelligence analysis and policy advice, the absence of which the British intelligence community has long believed weakened the business (for different reasons) in both the United States and the USSR (and its successor states). It was consistent with the Blair style for him to want material which presented a point of view, but there were distinct signs in early 2000 that the foreign, defence and intelligence communities were determined to resist this.[18]

And so they did — up to a point and with a certain finesse. Henceforth, about a third of JIC assessments carried a new 'implications' section of consequences that might flow if their

---

[16] Private information.

[17] Butler p. 87.

[18] Peter Hennessy, *The Prime Minister: The Office and Its Holders since 1945* (Penguin, 2000), p. 502.

analysis was right. Occasionally, a further 'if we are wrong' passage was added.[19]

So there matters rested when John Scarlett, the first MI6 officer to be so appointed to the post, became Chairman of the JIC but one week before the atrocity of 11 September 2001. Both Dearlove and Scarlett had been influenced by British intelligence history, especially that written by a former chairman of the JIC, Sir Percy Cradock. His study, *Know Your Enemy*,[20] of the performance of that committee and its staffs during the Cold War based on JIC files declassified at the Public Record Office left a strong impression on the two most influential intelligence figures in Mr Blair's decision-making circle in the run-up to the Iraq War — especially Cradock's section dealing with the Suez affair of 1956.[21] For the JIC, in the very first days of that crisis, warned its readers, including the Prime Minister, Sir Anthony Eden, of the 'international consequences' of a failure to achieve a swift, military victory over Colonel Nasser and Egypt 'both in the Arab states and elsewhere [which] might give rise to extreme embarrassment and cannot be forecast.'[22]

Scarlett and Dearlove were aware that the JIC had had a 'good Suez' but had not been heeded by their key reader in 10 Downing Street. They believed that all too often in the recent past, too, the intelligence product (costing about a billion pounds a year in 2000–1) had had an insufficient place in the Whitehall decision-making

---

[19] Peter Hennessy, 'Letter from Whitehall: Spooks mustn't be spinners', *The Tablet*, 6 September 2003.

[20] Percy Cradock, *Know Your Enemy: How the Joint Intelligence Committee Saw The World* (John Murray, 2002).

[21] Private information. For Cradock on Suez, see *Know Your Enemy*, pp. 109–34.

[22] National Archives, Public Record Office, CAB 158/25, JIC (56) 80 (Final) (Revise), 'Egyptian Nationalisation of the Suez Canal Company', 3 August 1956.

sun. Wherever the inner loops were, the two men were determined that they and their material would be within them. They were. It was quickly appreciated in post-9/11 Whitehall that thanks to Scarlett's and Dearlove's access to the Prime Minister, British intelligence had secured a more central place at the top decision-making tables to a degree unseen since the most perilous moments of the Cold War.

This aroused anxieties amongst other officials involved in the politico-military-intelligence world. One very experienced Cabinet Office figure, sensitive to accusations of a wider, creeping politicization of the crown services during the Blair premierships, called it the 'moth-and-the-flame' syndrome.[23] Such doubters felt vindicated when Butler reported and reinforced Lord Hutton's anxieties about such 'subconscious' factors by delineating plainly the degree to which SIS's validation procedures, the JIC's readiness to place excessive weight on one particular agent report out of Iraq on '45 minutes' readiness to deploy WMD and the manner in which such material was given to the Prime Minister in its raw state and unseen by the best experts in the Defence Intelligence Staff had amounted to a systems failure at the heart of British Intelligence.[24] As a result the September 2002 dossier, in Butler's unambiguous words, was flawed because 'more weight was placed on the intelligence than it could bear'[25] and that the pivotal '45 minute' claim should not have been included 'without stating what it was believed to refer to' (battlefield weapons — artillery rather than missiles) leading 'to suspicions that it had been included because of its eye-catching character.'[26]

---

[23] Private information.
[24] Butler pp. 99–102, 125, 137–8.
[25] Butler p. 154.
[26] Butler pp. 156–7.

Beyond their detailed revelations and judgements, there is a wider democratic point that emerges from both the Hutton and Butler reports. What in combination did they tell their readers that, but for the events which caused their inquiries to be commissioned, the public would not have been in a position to know or assess for themselves? The House of Commons itself was very vexed by this question after the Hutton Inquiry's witness roster, and the skill with which those witnesses were examined by professional lawyers before Lord Hutton, exposed a yawning gap between the Hutton hearings and both the reach and the forensic powers of the Commons Foreign Affairs Select Committee in June 2003 when it examined *The Decision to go to War in Iraq*.[27] Such was its sense of grievance that the Committee returned to this theme in March 2004.[28] The Liaison Committee, comprising all select committee chairmen, began its own inquiry into 'Select Committees after Hutton' in October 2003, including the possibility of helping MPs improve their questioning techniques through 'guidance or forensic training ... [or] ... [u]se of counsel for part of the questioning'.[29] The Liaison Committee pressed the Prime Minister strongly on this 'inquiry gap' when he appeared before them in July 2004, the week before Butler reported.[30]

---

[27] House of Commons Foreign Affairs Select Committee, *The Decision to go to War in Iraq*, HC 813–I, II and III (Stationery Office, 7 July 2003).

[28] House of Commons Foreign Affairs Select Committee, *Implications for the Work of the House and its Committees of the Government's Lack of Co-operation with the Foreign Affairs Committee's Inquiry into The Decision to go to War in Iraq*, HC 440 (Stationery Office, 18 March 2004).

[29] House of Commons Liaison Committee, *Scrutiny of Government: Select Committees after Hutton*, Note by the Clerks (undated). See also House of Commons Liaison Committee, *Annual Report for 2003*, HC 446 (Stationery Office, 11 March 2004), pp. 41–3.

[30] House of Commons Liaison Committee, *The Prime Minister*, Minutes of Evidence, 6 July 2004.

The Intelligence and Security Committee, which consists of parliamentarians drawn from both Houses but is *not* a select committee and operates within a ring of intelligence secrecy, fared much better than the Foreign Affairs Committee in terms of both witnesses and scope. Its September 2003 report on *Iraqi Weapons of Mass Destruction – Intelligence and Assessment* disclosed JIC anxieties in early 2003 that the chaos following a war in Iraq might trigger the nightmare of Al Qa'ida getting its hands on what WMD stocks might remain in that country.[31] Nonetheless, it later complained that 'eight relevant JIC papers' had not been made available to its members before drafting that report.[32]

But, taken together, even the most careful reading of these parliamentary reports by the concerned citizen would have left him or her incapable of reaching an informed judgement on the use of evidence inside Whitehall on the path to war. Thanks to Hutton and Butler we can go to the very heart of the matter of the use, or *non*-use, of evidence by our several governing tribes in Whitehall whether they be ministers, special advisers, permanent officials, or officers of the secret services. For myself, the amount of chaos that can sometimes surround real-time decision-taking was striking, as was the absence of the traditional, char-lady function by which I mean the careful taking of notes and writing of minutes which mop up after such discussions so that a proper record exists and subsequent, agreed actions are delineated.

It was the *degree* to which this had fallen into abeyance that surprised me. It was revealed most vividly when Jonathan Powell, the Prime Minister's Chief-of-Staff, gave evidence to Lord Hutton. At the time when No. 10 was concerned about both Dr Kelly and

---

[31] Intelligence and Security Committee, *Iraqi Weapons of Mass Destruction – Intelligence and Assessments*, Cm 5972 (Stationery Office, September 2003), p. 34.

[32] Intelligence and Security Committee, *Annual Report 2003–2004*, Cm 6240 (Stationery Office, June 2004), p. 25.

the press discovering that he was Andrew Gilligan's source, Mr Powell disclosed that of an average of 17 meetings a day in Downing Street, only three were minuted.[33] Lord Hutton's report stimulated action here. The Cabinet Secretary, Sir Andrew Turnbull, instructed that there should be a return to a very old technology. Minutes are back.[34]

Let us linger awhile in No. 10. In two key paragraphs (609 and 610[35]), the Butler Report hurls a bolt of lightning at the Blair style of government. Or, to be precise, at the difficulty the Prime Minister's very personal way of doing business caused the full Cabinet when it was required to exercise its collective responsibility on what Butler called 'the vital matter of war and peace.'[36] In careful language – and the paragraphs are all the more powerful because of it – the Butler Report suggests that the reliance on 'unscripted'[37] oral presentations from Mr Blair and the ministers in his inner group on Iraq, without supporting papers ('[e]xcellent quality papers were written by officials, but these were not discussed in Cabinet or Cabinet committee'[38]) meant that it was 'possible but ... obviously much more difficult'[39] for Cabinet ministers on the outer rim to test out the evidence and arguments of the inner circle even though discussion ranged over 24 meetings of the full Cabinet.[40]

Paradoxically, the impression within Whitehall was that when it came to diplomacy, war and Iraq, Tony Blair had been at his

---

[33] Hutton Inquiry transcripts for 18 August 2003.
[34] Peter Hennessy, *Rulers and Servants of the State: The Blair Style of Government 1997–2004*, (Office of Public Management, June 2004), p. 8.
[35] Butler pp. 147–8.
[36] Butler p. 148.
[37] Butler p. 147.
[38] Butler p. 147.
[39] Butler p. 147.
[40] Butler pp. 147–8.

most collegial, certainly more so than when dealing with domestic or economic affairs.[41] Here is a very well placed Downing Street insider in April 2003 on what he called 'The Prime Minister's Morning Meeting on Iraq.' Was it a proper Cabinet committee, I had asked.

> It's pretty damn close to it. It met pretty well daily at 8:30 with a fixed membership and prepared papers. If it had been called a Cabinet committee it would not have been any different.[42]

Dearlove and Scarlett met with the Prime Minister for 30 minutes before each meeting of what inevitably became known as the 'War Cabinet', fuelling still further the belief in Whitehall that the moth-and-the-flame syndrome was in operation.[43] Along with the Foreign Secretary, Jack Straw, the Defence Secretary, Geoff Hoon, the Chief of the Defence Staff, Sir Michael Boyce, and the Prime Minister's Foreign Affairs adviser, Sir David Manning, Dearlove and Scarlett were regular attenders at the 'War Cabinet'.[44]

Plainly Lord Butler and his Privy Counsellors did not believe that this inner group was as near as made no difference to a proper Cabinet committee. The Prime Minister was contrite on this criticism when he announced the four changes he would be making in response to Butler during the House of Commons debate about the report on 20 July 2004. Mr Blair accepted that it had been 'an informal group', and pledged that in future 'such a group, which brought together the key players required to work on operational military planning and developing the diplomatic

---

[41] Hennessy, *Rulers and Servants of the State*, p. 10.

[42] Private information.

[43] Hennessy, 'Spooks mustn't be spinners'.

[44] House of Commons, *Official Report*, 20 July 2004, col. 195.

strategy, will operate formally as an ad hoc Cabinet committee.'[45] (The three other changes Mr Blair promised involve, from 2005, the chairmanship of the JIC going to an official without expectation of a subsequent appointment in the crown service; the separation of analysis and advocacy in any future intelligence presentations to the public; and a review of SIS agent-report validation procedures and the place of the experts of the Defence Intelligence Staff in the overall internal hierarchy of esteem within the Whitehall intelligence community.[46])

In terms of proper collective responsibility, I think, the Labour Cabinet of 2002–3 was as much at fault as the Conservative Cabinet in late October 1956 when the Prime Minister, Sir Anthony Eden, told them that 'from secret conversations which had been held in Paris with representatives of the Israeli Government, it now appeared that the Israelis would not alone launch a full-scale attack against Egypt.'[47] You did not have to have had a career at the Government Communications Headquarters to decode that one. Eden's Cabinet did not press him on it as they should have done. And the consequences meant that for Whitehall, *not* 'doing an Anthony' was a kind of governing norm for a generation after.

In the long-term memory, the equivalent of the 1956 'collusion' is likely to be the '45 minutes' WMD readiness report. I never thought I would live to see the day when the public was told how many human agents SIS was running in a hard target country at a tricky time.[48] In the old days of 'need-to-know', very few were privy to such knowledge, and those who were had to sign several

---

[45] Ibid.

[46] Ibid.

[47] National Archives, Public Record Office, CAB 128/30, CM (56) 72, Confidential Annex, 23 October 1956. See also Peter Hennessy, *The Prime Minister: The Office and Its Holders since 1945* (Penguin, 2000), pp. 218–47.

[48] Butler pp. 100–4.

bits of paper before being told and were instructed to take such secrets with them to the grave.[49]

Thanks to Butler, we now know that it was the most alarmist *and* unproven of the handful of human sources in Iraq who supplied the '45 minute' material and that this provider was subsequently deemed unreliable.[50] As Sir Michael Quinlan's review of the purposes of British intelligence organizations for the Major Government stressed in 1994, such capabilities are vital for securing the last, opaque five to ten per cent of carefully guarded information from a target country.[51] Here human intelligence can range from pure gold to misleading dross and the toughest standards of validation must be applied to it. People who live in press offices or who work as special advisers are not normally faced with such stretching criteria as they fashion a press release about public service delivery or brief on a wheeze that might be used during Prime Minister's Questions in the House of Commons.

In the context of evidence-driven policy, the reason the United Kingdom sustains its 150-year tradition of permanent, politically neutral crown service is that the system needs such 'congenital snaghunters', as Hugh Dalton called his Treasury officials at particularly irritating moments in the early post-war years,[52] to work alongside ministers and politically-appointed special advisers whose driving purpose, as Enoch Powell liked to put it, is

---

[49] Private information.

[50] Butler pp. 101–2.

[51] This report has not been declassified but its essence can be savoured in Sir Michael Quinlan, 'The Future of Covert Intelligence', in Harold Shukman (ed.), *Agents for Change: Intelligence Services in the 21st Century* (St Ermin's Press/Little Brown, 2000), pp. 61–70.

[52] Peter Hennessy, *Whitehall* (Pimlico, 2001), p. 124.

'to give the people a tune to whistle'.[53] The Hutton Report was eloquent, as we have seen, about the possibility of 'subconscious' blowbacks from those whose skills lie in presentation affecting crown servants whose overriding duty is to speak truth unto power however inconvenient this, on occasion, might be.

But the biggest revelation from the combined Hutton/Butler lightning flash about the use of evidence in government is that the road to Baghdad was *not* paved with the intelligence product. The Butler Report shows that in the spring of 2002, when the Blair Government switched from containing Saddam to a policy designed 'to enforce disarmament [it] was not based on any new development in the current intelligence picture on Iraq.'[54] And, in the run-up to the war, the Attorney General, Lord Goldsmith (who eventually judged it legal without a further, specific United Nations' resolution authorizing the use of force[55]), warned his ministerial colleagues that 'there would be no justification for the use of force against Iraq on grounds of self-defence against an imminent threat.'[56]

Is there much left to learn about the twists and turns on the road to Baghdad post-Hutton and post-Butler? I think there *is* something concealed somewhere of particular relevance by which I mean the role of the UK's special forces in the months before the war for the purposes, in the jargon of the military, of 'shaping the battlefield'. If the Special Air Service or Special Boat Service teams found any Al-Hussein Missiles in the remote desert, (a) they would not have left them as they found them, and, (b) ministers on

---

[53] He used this metaphor on more than one occasion in conversation with the author. He had in mind, he explained, the Protestants 'whistling' the Catholic Stuarts off the throne in 1688 to the tune of *Lilibulero*.

[54] Butler p. 105.

[55] Butler Annex D, pp. 181–7.

[56] Butler p. 94.

the Prime Minister's inner group on Iraq would have known about it.

It is most unlikely that Iraq 2003 was the first recent conflict involving British troops which did not involve such prior precautions and preparations. There is not a whisper of this in Butler. But there was in the House of Lords almost exactly a year earlier in the reply from Lord Bach, Minister for Defence Procurement, to a carefully framed question from Lord Judd of Portsea, himself a former minister in both the Foreign and Commonwealth Office and the Ministry of Defence.

> LORD JUDD asked Her Majesty's Government:
> (a) what action they or their allies took in Iraq before the outbreak of the war to incapacitate all known scud missiles, similar weapons or other weapons of mass destruction;
> (b) how successful this action proved to be;
> (c) how many such weapons were incapacitated;
> (d) how many such weapons remained operational; and
> (e) by what date such action was completed.

> LORD BACH: As an integral part of the wider combat operation against Iraq, the Coalition undertook a variety of operations in order to neutralise the threats posed by the Iraqi Regime. I am withholding further details under Exemption 1 of the Code of Practice on Access to Government Information, which covers Defence, Security and International Relations.[57]

But the biggest gap (which, perhaps, should not be called that as it was beyond Lord Butler's remit if not Lord Hutton's) is motivation. If intelligence was not the driver on the road to Baghdad, what was? Seeking, in the title of Peter Riddell's fine

---

[57] House of Lords, *Official Report*, 17 July 2003, PQ Ref No. 4189N.

study,[58] to hug the Americans close whatever the evidence indicated? Not for Butler or Hutton to judge that one. I think the Prime Minister himself revealed the clue when he searched his conscience (his own phrase[59]) before the House of Commons on 14 July 2004, the day the Butler Report was published. Saddam, Mr Blair said,

> had no intention of ever co-operating fully with the [weapons] inspectors, and he was going to start up again ... I say further that if we had backed down in respect of Saddam, we would never have taken the stand that we needed to take on weapons of mass destruction, we would never have got the progress on Libya, for example, that we achieved and we would have left Saddam in charge of Iraq, with every malign intent and capability still in place, and with every dictator with the same intent everywhere immeasurably emboldened.[60]

This passage in Hansard made me go back to a note I took in the weeks after the war following a conversation with a specially central figure to whom I had put the question — what *was* that war for when one strips away all the inessentials? The answer?

> Iraq was the place where, if you were ever going to do anything about WMD that was it, because you *could* do something.[61]

Now back to Robin Butler's paragraph 427. In the spring of 2002, when containment of Saddam ceased to be the policy,

---

[58] Peter Riddell, *Hug Them Close: Blair, Clinton, Bush and the 'Special Relationship'* (Politicos, 2003; updated paperback edition 2004).
[59] House of Commons, *Official Report*, 14 July 2004, col. 1432.
[60] Ibid.
[61] Private information.

there was no recent intelligence that would itself have given rise to a conclusion that Iraq was of more immediate concern than the activities of some other countries,[62]

countries such as North Korea and Iran whose WMD capabilities Lord Butler helpfully analysed in chapter 2 of his report.[63]

Historians are not supposed to speculate. Nonetheless I shall finish by breaking this golden rule of my trade. Thanks to Hutton and Butler, as a well-placed UK intelligence officer put it in the days following Butler's publication, 'the doctrine of pre-emption has taken more than a kicking.'[64] I would agree with that while phrasing my conclusion slightly differently. No future Prime Minister and Cabinet will be able to take Britain into anything that is not a war of retaliation without being much more careful of both evidence and procedure. I also suspect that the day of the public intelligence dossier is done. *Not* 'doing a Tony' could prove just as powerful an impulse for tomorrow's Whitehall generations as 'not doing an Anthony' was for yesterday's. And, in that sense, the accumulation of the Hutton and Butler reports in the compost of collective memory will become a special kind of evidence in its own right.

The lightning flash may also inspire some cross-party parliamentary action. For example, the House of Commons could pass a resolution requiring the advice of the Attorney General on the legality of serious military action to be published in full before a Prime Minister and Cabinet took such a decision. The Commons Public Administration Select Committee, which in recent years has been very active on constitutional matters, including the use of

---

62 Butler p. 105.

63 Butler pp. 17–28.

64 Private information.

prerogative powers,[65] might consider drafting a War Powers Bill which, if enacted, would require a Prime Minister always to make 'the vital matter of war and peace' subject to a specific House of Commons vote. Nor will it have escaped the notice of that all-party committee, whose watching brief includes open government, that at least three-quarters of the material Hutton and Butler placed in the public domain fall into those intelligence-related areas that are exempt from disclosure under the terms of the Freedom of Information Act 2000 which comes into force on 1 January 2005.[66] There is at least a chance that Hutton and Butler together could lead to a significant and enduring shift in the balance of power between the Executive and the Legislature. Should this happen, the road to Baghdad really will have provided no end of a lesson learnt.

---

[65] *Taming the Prerogative: Strengthening Ministerial Accountability to Parliament,* HC 422, (Stationery Office, 2004).

[66] Peter Hennessy, 'The constitutional failure that has now been laid bare', *Guardian,* 24 July 2004.

Discussion

RICHARD WILSON

People will continue to discuss Iraq for a long time to come. Political debate will, of course, move on in time but the appetite to understand what happened is strong.

This may seem strange given that so much has been written about Iraq. In addition to what Peter Hennessy memorably calls the lightning flash of the reports by Lord Hutton and Lord Butler, there has been such a feast of words in the media that exhaustion should have set in long ago. But Iraq has touched deep nerves in our public life. Even issues which are normally of interest only to Secretaries of the Cabinet and a few commentators have become the stuff of headlines. I never expected to see a newsflash saying: 'Butler: concern about Government informality'.[67]

The Hutton and Butler reports tell us a great deal, as Peter Hennessy rightly says. They cannot tell us everything. There are other issues, not within the remit of either of them, where we still have only a dusty old 60 watt bulb to illuminate the evidence: issues about motivation, judgement and personality, for instance. And the story is not yet over, either in terms of domestic politics or international events. But we have a lot of evidence to be getting on with.

---

[67] It was swiftly replaced by 'Blair exonerated'.

To some degree the Butler and Hutton reports are complementary, casting light on each other. Consider for instance the Butler Committee's conclusion that the JIC's warnings on the limitations of the intelligence underlying its judgements were not made sufficiently clear in the dossier.[68] Let me read you an extract quoted in the Hutton Report:[69]

> ... it was an interesting week before the dossier was put out because there were so many things that people were saying well ... we're not sure about that, or they were happy about it being in but not expressed the way that it was, because you know the word-smithing is actually quite important and the intelligence community are a pretty cautious lot on the whole but once you get people putting it/presenting it for public consumption then of course they use different words. I don't think they're being wilfully dishonest I think they just think that's the way the public will appreciate it best. I'm sure you have the same problem as a journalist don't you, sometimes you've got to put things into words that the public will understand. ... In your heart of hearts you must realise sometimes that's not actually the right thing to say ... but it's the only way you can put it over if you've got to get it over in two minutes or three minutes ...

Those words are the words of Dr David Kelly speaking to Susan Watts in a tape-recorded conversation on 30 May 2003, the day after Mr Gilligan's famous broadcast. Dr Kelly may have been an uncorroborated single source but his words illuminate the Butler Committee's findings. His comments about the difficulty of reconciling truth and accuracy with the needs of modern media are of much wider relevance than just Iraq.

---

[68] Butler para. 465, p. 114.
[69] Hutton para. 36, p. 17, and Appendix 3.

There are two issues that arise out of the evidence of Dr Kelly that I would like to mention.

One is whether it would have been better, as soon as Dr Kelly came forward in early July 2003, to commission a formal investigation by an outsider into whether prima facie he had committed a disciplinary offence. Such a step would have been seen as harsh by some and politically hopeless by others; but it would have been due process. The virtue of due process is that it provides fairness for the individual and, by precluding prejudicial comment, some protection from the sort of political maelstrom into which Dr Kelly was drawn.[70]

There is a more fundamental point, namely the important distinction between management accountability of the kind I have just described and political accountability to Parliament. Lord Hutton found that Dr Kelly was in breach of the Official Code. That was a management matter for which he was accountable to his senior managers and department. It was different from political accountability under which his ministers (or senior civil servants answering on their behalf) could be required to account to Parliament for what had happened and how the breach was handled. These wires got crossed when Dr Kelly gave evidence to the Foreign Affairs Committee. A civil servant appearing before a Select Committee does so on behalf of his ministers, as the so-called Osmotherly Rules (on what an official can and cannot divulge or comment upon) make clear, not on his own behalf; and Select Committees are not constituted as disciplinary bodies. The situation contained the seeds of injustice whatever the rights and wrongs of Dr Kelly's behaviour; and, again, it lacked due process.

---

[70] There are precedents for this approach: for example, the investigation conducted by Sir David Yardley after the escape of IRA prisoners from Whitemoor prison in 1994.

I recognize of course that a Government in the grip of strong emotion is a fearsome thing, as indeed is a Prime Minister's Director of Communications, and I have sympathy for civil servants caught in the political storms of Iraq, pilloried in the media with no means of reply. My purpose is not to criticize but to suggest that what this evidence shows is that due process, whether it takes the form of the JIC's procedures or a department's disciplinary processes or the Osmotherly Rules or the practice of orderly collective government, is a good thing to hold on to in times of trouble for those whose job is to speak truth unto power.

This brings me to what is said in the Butler report about the 'informality and circumscribed character of the Government's procedures which ... risk reducing the scope for informed collective political judgement.'[71] It will come as no surprise that I agree with this judgement on the conduct of the government. Formal meetings and minute-taking for instance may seem bureaucratic and not 'modern'; but good minutes make sure that everyone knows what has been decided. The official machine responds well to a decision which is properly recorded by a No. 10 private secretary or the Cabinet Office. I believe there is a connection between proper processes and good government.

Different Prime Ministers have different ways of doing business and there is no 'right' way of running a Government. It is quite possible to reconcile due process with an informal style. But the risk is that informality can slide into something more fluid and unstructured, where advice and dissent may either not always be offered or else may not be heard. This is certainly a matter which engages collective responsibility. Prime Ministers are only as powerful as their colleagues allow them to be.

---

[71] Butler para. 611, p. 148.

The lessons from the Butler and Hutton reports are in a sense lessons which were already well known. Every generation has to learn the lessons of history or risk the pain of reinventing them. Whether those lessons have been learned, and for how long they will be remembered, is an important issue on the basis of this evidence. There are still rumbles of thunder in the Middle East.

Accuracy, Independence, and Trust

ONORA O'NEILL

Lord Hutton's task was to investigate the events surrounding the death of Dr David Kelly. His interpretation of his remit led him to focus on a range of accusations and counter-accusations. Government and the BBC had accused one another of inaccuracy, of making (partly) untruthful claims. More specifically, Andrew Gilligan's broadcast at 6.07 a.m. on 29 May 2003 was said to accuse the Government of *knowingly* adding a false claim to its *dossier* on Iraq, hence of lying to the public about one aspect of the grounds for invading Iraq.[1] Alastair Campbell, speaking for the Government, had accused the BBC of *wilfully* maintaining a false claim that Government had done this in the face of evidence that it had not, of reiterating the claim and refusing to check its truth or falsity.[2] Lord Hutton concluded that the BBC's stronger accusation did not stick,[3] but that the Government's weaker accusation stuck.[4]

The accusations, if substantiated, were likely to damage public trust in the Government or in the BBC, or in both. Lord Hutton's findings suggest on the surface that trust in the BBC should have been more seriously damaged. However, some months later, trust in the BBC appeared less damaged than trust in Government. There were no doubt lots of reasons for this: the BBC was more trusted than Government before the Hutton report was published.[5]

---

[1] Lord Hutton, *Report of the Inquiry into the Circumstances Surrounding the Death of David Kelly C.M.G.*, HC 247 (2004) (hereafter Hutton), para. 32, pp. 12–13. The broadcast included the words 'what we've been told by one of the senior officials in charge of drawing up that dossier was that, actually the government probably erm, knew that that forty five minute figure was wrong, even before it decided to put it in.' Subsequently many in the BBC defended the broadcast on the grounds that it had merely reported an accusation, but had not accused; I shall return to this point.

[2] Hutton para. 63, p. 41. Campbell also accused the BBC of subsequently lying about what they had done: Hutton para. 265, p. 178.

[3] Hutton para. 467 (1), pp. 319–21.

[4] Hutton para. 467 (3), pp. 321–3.

[5] http://www.mori.com/polls/2003/iraq4-top.shtml

The BBC apologised after the Report was published[6] and Government did not (arguably, since the central accusation against Government had not been substantiated, no apology was called for). The Chairman of Governors and the Director-General of the BBC resigned, and ministers did not (again, arguably, the Report had not given them reason to do so). More significantly, I suspect, reports of levels of trust and mistrust in Government and in the BBC reflect a wide range of issues, most of them unrelated to the events covered in the Hutton Report.

This might suggest that the Hutton Report can't tell us much about public trust and mistrust. However, that conclusion may reflect too ready an assumption that trust and mistrust are no more than rather general attitudes of the sort that pollsters investigate, and that they float free of evidence. This can no doubt happen: trust and mistrust can be blind and unevidenced. But usually they are not.

Placing and refusing trust

Trust is a practical matter: we decide to place or to refuse trust in others' words and actions, in their claims and commitments. In an ideal world we would place trust in true claims and in commitments that are followed up in action, and refuse trust to false claims and to commitments that are not followed up in action. But since claims and commitments do not wear their truth or reliability on their face, we have to judge cases. More precisely,

---

[6] The apology may have been retracted in comments made by Greg Dyke and Andrew Gilligan after the publication of the Butler report. Greg Dyke is quoted as saying 'I would defend that decision (to broadcast Dr Kelly's concerns) forever.' http://news.bbc.co.uk/1/hi/uk_politics/3895135.stm

we have to judge specific claims and specific commitments to action on the basis of such evidence as we can assemble for them. Since we place or refuse trust in *specific* truth claims and *specific* commitments to action, we often — and very reasonably — trust persons and institutions in some matters, but refuse to trust them in others.

Placing and refusing trust do not demand *proof* that others' claims are true, or *guarantees* that they will honour their commitments. Proofs and guarantees marginalize trust by eliminating the context in which it is needed. Nevertheless, trust is evidence-based. That is why we are generally better at judging whether it is reasonable to trust *specific* truth claims or *specific* commitments, than we are at judging whether a person or institution is to be trusted — or mistrusted — across the board. It can be entirely sensible to trust some, but not other claims made by a journalist — or a politician. It is one thing to judge whether a claim that Iraq had ready-to-use WMDs is likely to be true or false; another to judge (whether or not the claim about WMDs is true) that those who made the claim lacked reasonable evidence; a third to judge (whether or not the claim about WMDs is true) that those who made it both lacked reasonable evidence and knew that they lacked reasonable evidence, so were lying. For Andrew Gilligan's initial claim[7] to stick he did not have to judge or state whether or not Iraq had WMDs ready to hand. But he did have to judge and indicate the grounds both for thinking that Government had lacked reasonable evidence for claiming that Iraq had WMDs

---

[7] Even if Andrew Gilligan's broadcast could have been defended as reporting allegations about Government made by a reliable source, rather than as making allegations about Government (a move tried by the BBC), these distinctions would be important. See below.

ready to hand, and for thinking that they had known that they lacked reasonable evidence. In saying that he had to judge these matters, I do not mean that he needed proof: he needed only reasonable evidence.[8]

The demands of accuracy

Is this epistemological fussiness just an occupational deformation of philosophers, and irrelevant to journalism and public life? I don't think so. Both Government and the media accept that (with very rare exceptions) their truth claims should aim to be *intelligible* and *accurate,* and their commitments *intelligible* and *reliable* (the latter is evidently of greater importance in judging governments; the media make many truth claims, but few commitments). The requirement that truth claims and commitments be intelligible to intended audiences may seem banal, although it is quite often flouted (for example, by those in thrall to communication strategies or to ideals of political correctness). However, I shall take this demand as uncontroversial. Requirements for accuracy and for reliability introduce more complex considerations. The demand for accuracy in communication is central to any consideration of the Hutton Report.

A demand for accuracy is not a demand that anybody communicate 'the whole truth', or that they communicate without selectivity, or that they achieve high precision. Nor is it a demand for objectivity, which might be understood as combining

---

[8] This is not to say that the truth of claims about Iraq's WMDs was wholly irrelevant. Those who make true claims relying on evidence they believe to be inadequate are likely to be judged less harshly than those who make false claims relying on evidence they believe to be inadequate.

requirements for accuracy with requirements for coverage, or even for impartiality. A commitment to accuracy is simply a matter of seeking to avoid false claims. It is a central part even of the least demanding press codes, such as the Press Complaints Commission *Code of Practice*.[9] It is, of course, also a central element in the more demanding set of standards required in Public Service Broadcasting and basic to the *Producers' Guidelines* of the BBC,[10] under which Andrew Gilligan was working. Equally, accuracy is constantly invoked as a standard in Government communication, and was taken as central in the post-Hutton *Independent Review of Government Communications*, chaired by Bob Phillis, that reported in January 2004.[11] Nobody advocates or condones inaccuracy. Indeed, it is hard to see how the issues covered in the Hutton Report could have led to any dispute between the Government and the BBC if it had not been common ground that accuracy matters.

Clearly a commitment to accuracy cannot demand exceptionless success. Neither Government nor the media, nor any of us, are going to achieve that. The only way to ensure total accuracy would be to avoid all communication. It is not just that those who work at some speed — not only journalists — often have to deliver before they can check all their claims thoroughly.

---

[9] Accuracy is the first requirement of the Press Complaints Commission *Code of Practice*, which demands that: 'i) The Press must take care not to publish inaccurate, misleading or distorted information, including pictures'; and 'ii) A significant inaccuracy, misleading statement or distortion once recognised must be corrected, promptly and with due prominence, and — where appropriate — an apology published.'
See http://www.pcc.org.uk/cop/cop.asp
[10] *Producers' Guidelines: The BBC's values and standards* (London: BBC, 2000), http://www.bbc.co.uk/info/policies/producer_guides/pdf/section1.pdf
[11] http://www.gcreview.gov.uk/

The deeper reasons why we cannot demand total accuracy are that evidence is often incomplete, that available evidence tracks truth imperfectly, and that even those who take care in making truth claims track evidence imperfectly. Even those who work slowly and methodically may get things wrong on occasion. Nor is scrupulous honesty enough to secure accuracy: truthfulness is helpful for avoiding inaccuracy, but cannot guarantee truth, or even accuracy on specific points. So a commitment to accuracy would be incomplete and unrealistic unless it included a commitment to correct inadvertent inaccuracy, as demanded by the second clause in the Press Complaints Commission *Code of Practice*.

We may all be fallible, but there are nevertheless differences between communication that aims at accuracy, communication that is casual about accuracy, and communication that is deliberately inaccurate. Communication that aims at accuracy uses tried and tested procedures: the routines of fact-checking and verifying sources, of checking the record and the calculations, of submitting work to others' judgement, of selecting and testing the caveats and qualifications, are all of them part and parcel of a commitment to accuracy. Procedures for securing a good level of accuracy are typically embedded in professional and institutional processes, including journalistic, editorial, administrative and managerial processes. Following these procedures can be boring, but given the inevitable incompleteness and untidiness of available evidence, these routines are needed if we are to achieve a reasonable level of accuracy in making truth claims about complex matters, and most urgently needed where the evidence is hardest to assess. They entrench ways of ensuring that claims are limited and qualified, that communication does not mislead by going beyond that evidence. Where the evidence is thin, it is possible to say so; where a source is untested, that can be made plain; where a conclusion is no more than speculative, that can be emphasized;

where there is a gap in the information, that can be pointed out rather than slurred; and so on. Routines to achieve these standards are part and parcel of good journalistic and editorial procedures, of good administrative and civil service process, and more generally of good professional practice.

Where inaccuracy comes to light at a later stage, there can be equally routine ways of dealing with it. Corrections can be made; caveats that were omitted can be added; inaccuracy that has misled others may be remedied. Deliberate inaccuracy that has defamed or injured others may require weightier remedies, such as retraction, apology, compensation — or resignation.

Institutions and professionals that aim at accuracy in their communication — among them Government and the media — need reliable routines of these sorts. Accurate communication needs attentive and organized efforts to avoid communication that misinforms and misleads. Mere freedom of expression will not be enough for discovering truth, or for maintaining accuracy. As the late Bernard Williams noted:

> In institutions that are expressly dedicated to finding out the truth, such as universities, research institutes, and courts of law, speech is not at all unregulated. People cannot come in from outside, speak when they feel like it, make endless irrelevant, or insulting, interventions, and so on; they cannot invoke a right to do so, and no-one thinks that things would go better in the direction of truth if they could.[12]

Both the disciplines of accurate reporting and editorial control, and the disciplines needed for accurate communication within and by Government are demanding. Both must include and maintain

---

[12] Bernard Williams, *Truth and Truthfulness* (Princeton, NJ: Princeton University Press, 2002), p. 217.

processes for avoiding, detecting and correcting inaccuracy, in order to ensure that (a reasonable level of) accuracy is ultimately achieved, even if there are initial defects.

Process and accuracy

Parts of the Hutton Report examine the BBC's journalistic, editorial and managerial processes. Other parts focus (to a lesser degree) on the BBC's system of governance. Since the Report did not look at the work of the Intelligence Services, it did not consider the adequacy of the processes on which they (or other parts of government) relied: a central theme of the Butler Report.[13] The Hutton Report found that the processes used by the BBC in this case did not show a sufficient commitment to accuracy. The evidence did not support a claim that Government had knowingly inserted a false claim in the dossier. Nor did it support Andrew Gilligan's claim that a knowledgeable source, later identified as Dr Kelly, had told him that Government had done so. Claims that the source had said this could not be clearly supported either by Gilligan's notes and summaries[14] (they come in various versions, and are hard to follow), or by Dr Kelly's statements to his line managers[15] and to the House of Commons Foreign Affairs Committtee,[16] or by other statements made by Dr Kelly.

---

[13] *Review of Intelligence on Weapons of Mass Destruction. Report of a Committee of Privy Counsellors,* http://www.butlerreview.org.uk/report/

[14] Hutton paras 229–248, pp. 155–167.

[15] For example: Dr Kelly wrote to his line manager Dr Bryan Wells stating on 30 June 2003 'I made no allegations or accusations about any issue related to the dossier or the Government's case for war', Hutton para. 46, pp. 25–27. He told the Foreign Affairs Select Committee that he did not believe that he was Andrew Gilligan's main source, Hutton para. 103, p. 62. An internal MoD assessment of the evidence on 4 July 2003 concluded: 'if there were a single

The lack of clear evidence that Dr Kelly had in fact told Andrew Gilligan that the Government had knowingly inserted a false claim into the dossier on Iraq's weapons of mass destruction undermined the main line of defence used by the BBC. This defence claimed that the BBC had made no allegations against Government, but had rather reported a source's allegations against Government.[17] If Andrew Gilligan had not reported his source accurately, this line of defence would fail. Within the BBC it was widely assumed that Gilligan had reported accurately.[18] However, as the row between Government and BBC developed, some of those closest to the *Today* programme expressed doubts about Gilligan's standards and procedures. On 27 June 2003 — ten days before the Governors took a stand that assumed that Gilligan had been accurate — Kevin Marsh, editor of the *Today* programme, wrote to Stephen Mitchell, the Head of Radio News. He expressed worries that Andrew Gilligan's work was characterized by 'loose use of language and lack of judgement in some of his phraseology' and about his 'loose and distant relationship with Today',[19] and suggested extensive changes in the way Gilligan's work should be managed.

Would the BBC's line of defence have been convincing if Andrew Gilligan had reported his source accurately? It would

---

source for Gilligan's information, then it was not Kelly', Hutton para. 50, p. 32.

[16] Hutton para. 103, pp. 59–67.

[17] This line of defence was used by Greg Dyke in answering Lord Hutton, Hutton para. 290, pp. 201–5, and by Gavyn Davies in writing to other Governors on 6 July 2003, Hutton para. 270, pp. 181–82.

[18] That this was an *assumption* rather a *conclusion* based on considering the evidence is made entirely clear in the Chairman's communication with Governors, Hutton para. 270, p. 181.

[19] Hutton para. 284, p. 195.

certainly have been a far better line of defence, but it would still not have been unproblematic. The media are taken to report the news, and where they report an unsubstantiated opinion or an allegation, a commitment to accuracy demands that they make this wholly explicit.   Hence the care and caveats with which the BBC *Producers' Guidelines* address the issue of single sourcing. To meet the required standards, Andrew Gilligan would have had to report accurately what Dr Kelly had said, to take very explicit steps to show that he was only reporting an allegation, and to make the case for relying on a single source. Otherwise listeners could not have told that the BBC was reporting an accusation rather than accusing Government.

But this was not what happened. Andrew Gilligan accepted under cross-examination on 17 September 2003 that he had not reported accurately. He was asked '... when you said that the Government probably knew that it [the 45 minutes figure] was wrong, you were actually saying, whether you intended to or not, that they were dishonest, were you not?' He replied '... the allegation that I intended to make [sic: *allegation* not *report of allegation*] was of spin, but as I say, I do regard those words as imperfect and I should not have said them.'[20] Shortly thereafter he said 'The intention was to report what Dr Kelly had told me; and I regret that on those two occasions I did not report entirely carefully and accurately what he had said. My error was to ascribe that statement to him when it was actually a conclusion of mine.'[21]

What could the BBC have done to secure greater accuracy? Lord Hutton found specifically that the BBC failed to exercise editorial control, in that there was no check of Andrew Gilligan's report before it was broadcast unscripted.[22] A requirement that all

---

[20] Hutton para. 245, p. 165.
[21] Hutton para. 246, p. 167.
[22] Hutton para. 284, p. 195.

broadcasting to be scripted and checked may be unrealistic, although perhaps less unrealistic for broadcasting on very serious matters. But plausibly the editorial failing was rather more general, a matter of Gilligan's 'loose and distant relationship with Today', of his 'loose use of language and lack of judgement'.[23]

Lord Hutton also criticized BBC management and the Governors for failing to take steps to check the content or the accuracy of the 6.07 broadcast after receiving a complaint. Both BBC senior management and the Governors repeatedly defended their processes on the *assumption* that Gilligan had reported his source accurately, that he had reported an allegation and that he had not accused the Government of lying. They also pointed out repeatedly that the Government had made wider charges against the BBC, and insisted on the importance of standing up for BBC independence. However, on 17 September Mr Greg Dyke agreed when questioned that, when replying to Alastair Campbell on 27 June along these lines, he had not yet read Andrew Gilligan's notes, and that he had subsequently realized that the basis for claiming that Gilligan had reported a source accurately was weak.[24] The evidence for reluctance within the BBC to check the accuracy of what had been broadcast at 6.07 is overwhelming: it is not a fiction created by Alastair Campbell's energetic — sometimes frenetic — letters to the BBC. It consists mainly of BBC internal documents written by editors, by BBC management, by managers and by the Chairman of the Governors. These documents show that those at the most senior levels in the BBC assumed, but did

---

[23] Hutton para. 284, p. 195.

[24] 'I think if I had been able to go through Andrew Gilligan's notes in some detail and gone through them with him in some detail, we might have got to a point where we realised these were not comments that were directly attributable to Dr Kelly; and clearly I regret that.' Hutton para. 290, pp. 202–3.

not check, that the 6.07 broadcast had reported an allegation accurately.

Independence and accuracy

This failure to check the evidence by an institution so strongly committed to accuracy is striking. So are the reasons given for not doing so. Ostensibly both BBC management and the Governors felt that if they did not defend the broadcast about which Government had complained, they would be failing to defend the independence of the BBC. Mr Gavyn Davies wrote to other Governors on 1 July 2004 putting the point dramatically: 'If the BBC allows itself to be bullied by this sort of behaviour from No 10, I believe that this could fatally damage the trust that the public places in us. ... This is a moment for the Governors to stand up and be counted. ... [W]e must not give any ground which threatens the fundamental independence of our news output, or suggests that the Governors have buckled to government pressure.'[25] In the subsequent meeting of the Governors on 6 July 2003,[26] there is evidence of ample unease about the procedures that had been followed, or not followed, and about the fact that the Governors had not checked the accuracy of Gilligan's report for themselves, but the meeting nevertheless decided that the *Producers' Guidelines* had been adhered to. This position was maintained despite the fact that a number of well-placed people in the BBC had been worried about the quality of Gilligan's broadcast for some time. It was reasserted in the statement made by the BBC on 20 July after the death of Dr Kelly, which includes the statement: 'The BBC believes

---

[25] Hutton para. 269, p. 180.
[26] Hutton para. 272, pp. 182–9.

we accurately interpreted and reported the factual information obtained by us during interviews with Dr Kelly.'[27]

The BBC in effect adopted a position in which the demands of independence and for accuracy were thought of as opposed. Yet the supposed conflict between the demands of independence and of accuracy is bogus. A principal reason why the BBC's institutional independence is to be taken so seriously is in order to secure a reliable and accurate source of information for citizens, that is not controlled by Government or by business. Attempts to subordinate accuracy to independence undermine the case for independence. Lord Hutton judged defence of independence and commitment to accuracy compatible when he ruled that while 'The Governors were right to take the view that it was their duty to protect the independence of the BBC', they should also have 'recognised more fully than they did that their duty to protect the independence of the BBC was not incompatible with giving proper consideration to whether there was validity in the Government's complaints.'[28]

How and why did the BBC and those who supported its stance come to see the dispute as a challenge to BBC independence? Part of the reason was no doubt that Alastair Campbell had subjected the BBC to a barrage of complaints, with the understandable result that journalists, editors and managers were fed up with him. This may explain the initial BBC failure to check the accuracy of the Gilligan broadcast; but it hardly explains (or justifies) the persistent refusal to consider whether the complaint had any basis. Seen with hindsight, there was an alternative approach whereby the complaint was promptly investigated and any aspects of the report for which no reasonable

---

[27] Hutton para. 159, p. 104.
[28] Hutton para. 291, p. 213.

evidence could be found in Andrew Gilligan's notes (and other sources) were identified and corrected by the BBC. That would not have been much of a 'climb down', it would have given evidence of serious commitment to accuracy, and it would not have compromised independence. Resignations would have been unnecessary. Public trust would have been respected rather than damaged.

Yet the BBC persisted in construing government complaints about inaccuracy as an attack on its independence, and so as a matter on which there could be no retreat. They did so despite the fact that it is hard to find evidence that anyone else, including Government, was challenging the BBC's independence. Alastair Campbell indeed made it explicit that the complaints he was voicing did not challenge BBC independence.[29] The consistency with which the BBC avoided looking into the accuracy of the 6.07 broadcast until the Hutton Inquiry posed pointed questions suggests a very particular view of independence and of its importance for creating and maintaining trust.

Independence and trust

Why did senior people in the BBC feel that *any* move to check the accuracy of the 6.07 broadcast would compromise their independence and 'could fatally damage the trust that the public places in us'?[30] Clearly the conception of independence that lies

---

[29] He wrote to the BBC Governors before the meeting of 6 July stating that 'I note from press cuttings that the BBC views my complaint as an attack upon the independence of the BBC. I want to assure you that is not the case. I respect the BBC's independence. I believe the BBC is one of the country's greatest assets and I have long been an admirer of its ethos, much of its journalism and many of its journalists.' Hutton para. 271, pp. 181–2.
[30] See above n. 25.

behind this thought must be more radical than the robust *institutional* independence that statute, charter, licence fee and tradition secure for the BBC — which was not under threat. Some of the comments suggest those who took a more *radical* conception of independence saw it as more or less unconditional, in the way that individual rights to freedom of expression are more or less unconditional.

Freedom of expression has traditionally been seen as a right of *individuals*, and as distinct from media freedom and independence. For example, in *On Liberty* John Stuart Mill argues that individual liberty includes 'absolute freedom of opinion and sentiment on all subjects, practical or speculative, scientific, moral, or theological', and that 'liberty of expressing and publishing opinions' is 'practically inseparable' from 'freedom of opinion and sentiment'.[31] The classical arguments for a more or less unconditional view of individual freedom of expression do not require individuals to communicate accurately, or to achieve even meagre epistemic standards. Individuals may express false or unwarranted beliefs; they may be ignorant or crazy, but their freedom of expression will be restricted only by limited requirements not to endanger, defame or incite.

The twentieth century Declarations and Conventions on Human Rights also proclaim more or less unconditional rights to freedom of expression for individuals. For example, *Article 19* of the United Nations' *Universal Declaration of Human Rights* runs:

> Everyone has the right to freedom of opinion and expression; this right includes freedom to hold opinions without interference and to

---

[31] John Stuart Mill, *On Liberty* (1859), in *On Liberty and other writings*, ed. Stefan Collini (Cambridge: Cambridge University Press, 1989), p. 15.

seek, receive and impart information and ideas through any media and regardless of frontiers.[32]

The European Convention on Human Rights also proclaims a more or less unconditional freedom of expression as a right *of individuals*. *Article 10* begins with the words:

> Everyone has the right to freedom of expression. This right shall include freedom to hold opinions and to receive and impart information and ideas without interference by public authority and regardless of frontiers.[33]

Freedom of expression does not provide a good model for press freedom. There are powerful arguments for press freedom, but they are different. They typically stress the importance of a free press for citizens and for democracy, and in doing so implicitly reject the view that the media have unconditional freedom of expression or unconditional independence. For if the media had unconditional freedom of expression, they would have no obligation to inform citizens accurately, let alone to assist them when they seek to 'impart information and ideas'. If the media had more or less unconditional freedom of expression, they could use their power to obstruct individuals' chances of expressing their opinions, or to hinder the expression of certain sorts of opinions. Convincing arguments for media freedom do not model it on freedom of expression, but as freedom linked to a requirement to inform citizens and others accurately.

---

[32] *Universal Declaration of Human Rights*, adopted by the General Assembly of the United Nations in 1948, http://www.un.org/Overview/rights.html
[33] *Convention for the Protection of Human Rights and Fundamental Freedoms*, http://www.echr.coe.int/Convention/webConvenENG.pdf

Yet it has become increasingly common to equate media freedom with freedom of expression. For example, the campaigning group *Article 19*,[34] depict media freedom as a form of freedom of expression. They describe their campaign for media freedom as 'the global campaign for freedom of expression'.[35] Those who equate freedom of expression with media freedom are short of arguments. Powerful institutions — whether governments or the media — would no doubt often find the radical independence that is implied by a more or less unconditional view of freedom of expression convenient, and might be tempted to claim it. But if they enjoyed the same more or less unconditional rights to freedom of expression that the charters accord to individuals, they would not be bound by any obligation to aim for accuracy, let alone for more demanding standards. They would be as free to misinform as to inform citizens, to subvert as to support public debate and democracy. A conception of media freedom or independence that floats free of any obligation to aim for accuracy is therefore quite implausible. Such radical independence would undermine any basis for members of the public to judge where to place and where to refuse trust.

The media do not claim explicitly that they should enjoy more or less unconditional freedom of expression. On the contrary, their very acceptance of codes and standards shows that they think media freedom is rightly limited in ways that individuals' freedom of expression is not. Yet — as the Hutton Report makes clear — some parts of the media sometimes act as if they had a sufficiently

---

[34] They take their name from article 19 of the *Universal Declaration of Human Rights*, which proclaims *individual* rights to freedom of expression.
[35] http://www.article19.org/

wide freedom of expression to dispense them from at least some implications of a commitment to accuracy. It is not hard to see why this discrepancy between official view and actual conduct arises.

An exaggerated conception of independence that subordinates accuracy can be tempting in many ways — to government, to the media and to others. Commitments to accuracy can stand in the way of a good story, of persuading others to view things in a certain way, of 'news management' and of spin. A culture of public relations and spin, of hype and exaggeration, lurks in the interstices of the events into which Lord Hutton inquired. These are all of them ways of marginalizing or reducing commitments to accuracy, and each damages the prospect of placing or refusing trust intelligently. Once public documents or reporting to the public are seen as modes of persuasion, accuracy as well as assessability may be subordinated to other agendas. The public may be left without the means to assess what they read or hear, or to check or challenge its truth. At that point all attempts to place or to refuse trust intelligently will be frustrated, and the public are left with little option but to veer blindly between suspicion and credulity.

I do not think that the central parts of the Hutton Report reveal much that is new about the harm that can be caused when spin, persuasion, and public relations agendas dominate public communication. But in its interstices there are many glimpses of a culture of 'strategic' communication by Government and others, and of a culture that permits and fosters ways of reporting news that shade into ways of making and shaping news. This is a culture which makes it easy to lose sight of the reasons why communication has to be intelligible, accurate, and assessable by its audiences if it is to provide a basis for them to place or refuse trust intelligently.

Process and trust

The procedures that underlie and make a reality of a commitment to accurate communication have two benefits. The first, on which I have concentrated, is that well-used procedures provide a (fallible) means to accurate conclusions. They cannot guarantee accuracy: evidence is never complete; even good evidence does not track truth perfectly. Sometimes there is little evidence for accurate claims, or considerable evidence for inaccurate claims.

The second advantage of procedures for securing accuracy is that they can be incorporated into communication in ways that provide others with the evidence they need to judge which claims are accurate and which commitments reliable. If we are to place and refuse trust in others' claims or commitments with discrimination, it is not enough that they make accurate claims and reliable commitments. They must also provide others with the means of assessing the truth of their claims and the reliability of their commitments. Fortunately, the very procedures that help secure accuracy will, if incorporated into communication with others, offer (fallible) means for others to assess accuracy and reliability, and so a (fallible) basis for placing or refusing trust.

Many of the documents disclosed in the Hutton Report, and much of the questioning and cross-examination, rely on procedures that help secure accuracy, and that provide others with means to judge whether and how far to trust what they read, see or hear. The Report includes careful minutes of meetings; letters between senior office-holders; testimony before parliamentary committees; answers given in cross-examination. Repeatedly there is care and hesitation to choose the right word, to make the necessary distinctions, to note what an individual knew and did not know at a particular moment, to include the qualifications and caveats. The Report is full of the speech of people who do not view accuracy about complex matters as simple, and who are trained in procedures that support accuracy. Nevertheless, some of them not merely made claims that turned out to be inaccurate (hardly surprising given that accuracy is demanding), but dispensed with procedures that are important for securing accuracy. (The Butler Report on the processes by which intelligence was assessed and published comments on parallel issues.)

With all this talent and training in communicating accurately, what went wrong? Was the whole affair just a reflection of the unavoidable looseness of fit between accuracy and the evidence for accuracy? That is unlikely to be the whole answer, in that sensitivity to that looseness of fit is exactly what training in the disciplines and procedures used for securing accuracy and communicating accurately is designed to deal with. Is it a case of a weak link in a chain, for example of simple failure in standards for reporting? That cannot be the full story, in that the BBC's *subsequent* handling of the issues continued to underplay the importance of accuracy and of procedures for maintaining and checking accuracy, in the name of an implausible conception of independence. That was what allowed the conflict to escalate. Beyond these failings there lies, I believe, a wider tendency to exaggerate or misconceive the forms of independence that the media require, at the cost of giving short shrift to accuracy and to evidence needed if citizens are to place and refuse trust intelligently.

So does the Hutton Report provide us with reasons not to place trust in the BBC? Were the events the inquiry investigated only an aberration in high places, or are they symptomatic of the way the BBC now works? I will leave the last word to a reporter from Radio Ulster who found the events that emerged in the Hutton Inquiry painful and barely credible. He said to me shortly after the death of Dr Kelly: 'Over here we are taught to check our facts and check our facts — after all, somebody's life might depend on it.' His words hovered in the air. That, I hope, is the authentic voice of the BBC.

Discussion

JOHN LLOYD

Onora O'Neill has been foremost among scholars in tackling directly the issue of trust in the media. Like most others, I became aware of her interest when she gave the Reith Lectures two years ago on the theme of Trust, and devoted one of the six to the media.[1] She has continued the interest: and I hope she'll do more. There are few lines of enquiry my profession need more.

This is because we have become so powerful. We are the major writers of the narratives of society — the more so as other institutions with rival stories to tell and lessons to teach (churches, the military, trade unions, even families) decline in influence and coherence in the face of media — especially television — which account for the largest single chunk of most peoples' leisure time. Of course, most people do not spend most of that time watching news media: but they tend to watch what they do of the news and current affairs in the same space as everything else — a point I'll come back to.

The key elements I take from her essay, and on which I want to comment briefly, are, first, that media tend to show independence by opposition to the Government of the day — indeed, to define the first by the exercise of the second; and that

---

[1] Onora O'Neill, *A Question of Trust: The BBC Reith Lectures* (Cambridge University Press, 2002).

110

this can be destructive of trust. Hutton's account of what the BBC management did after the complaint from Alastair Campbell, then the Prime Minister's Director of Communications, on the 29 May 2003 broadcast by Andrew Gilligan — based on BBC documents and emails — shows that the executives did care more about opposition than about accuracy. In this, I believe, the BBC shares a certain temper of the times without questioning it. It has been for some time — predating by some years the Labour Government — a gradually strengthening view among reporters that Governments, and most public officials, should be approached not with proper scepticism but with open cynicism. The themes of cynicism are rehearsed by newspapers to the point where they become received wisdom — dominant among them that Governments spin, which easily elides into view that Government lies — and become so ingrained that the need for proof that Governments actually do lie is seen as almost beside the point. It is I think because of that dominant view that the BBC so lightly broadcast the fact that the Prime Minister lied to get the country to go to war, and so stalwartly defended the broadcast when challenged. It seemed obvious that it was telling the truth and that Government was lying.

Second, Onora O'Neill has talked of the need for proof and accuracy, and if the proof turns out to be wrong and the accuracy thus called into question, for a culture of correction and apology. We know that the *New York Times* has apologized at great length for the false reports of Jayson Blair; and then apologized once more, under less pressure to do so, for reporting on preparations for the Iraq war which, it said, were too lightly investigated, while the administration statements were taken too much at face value. The BBC also apologized for the Gilligan broadcast, though it took longer to do so; and its former Chairman and its former Director-General have both let it be known that they don't think it did anything wrong — a view shared by quite a number of its staff. In fact, the British media haven't got much of a culture of correcting: only one paper, I believe — the *Guardian* — has appointed a reader's editor, or ombudsman; while the Press Complaints Commission, the body to which complaints are referred, has a limited remit to investigate.

She reminds us that other professions — law and the academy — have quite tightly regulated their search for the truth, and regard the regulation as intrinsic to that search. We regard it as an inhibition to discovering the truth, and that is misguided. I share this bias only to the extent that I don't think inaccuracies should — beyond the law of libel — be made the subject of legislation. First, in a practical way: regulation or prohibition on the media would be tested to attempted destruction — as the BBC tested to destruction the ban on interviews with IRA members, by interviewing IRA men and then using actors' voices to substitute for the real ones. Second, unless we in the media, and people in public life generally, raise the media culture, then legislation is probably useless — unless it were carefully crafted laws on privacy.

Her point on 24-hour news and its attendant witterings is right: it reminds us that at one time those charged with putting out the news would sometimes declare there was none — and that they could be right. However, 24-hour news doesn't permit of a vacuum, and thus comment and bias fill the spaces between meagre facts and old briefings. And thus we don't know what to trust, since we don't know what the reporter knows which lies behind his or her comments — whether it's a briefing or knowledge whose source can't be divulged, or just a space-filler with no foundation.

There is a vast amount of material now in the public domain: more will come when the Freedom of Information Act comes into force next year. How is it to be assessed? For sure, it will contain much that could be damaging to this and past Governments. Is that because this Government is worse than previous Governments? Or because we have not known how bad previous Governments were, and this one is in the same despicable mould? Or is it how Government is? Who will do the assessing of this information — and how will it be understood? It does not need a belief in a golden age of reporting to believe it is not being done well now.

Onora O'Neill says, on giving a list of issues affecting our trust, that there will be others than those she's mentioned. And I want to flag up three. One, on which she does touch, is the matter of Government persuasion — or what's known as spin. The present Government was tremendously good at spin — it gave very convincing narratives about itself, and about the then Conservative Government, when in opposition. It grasped a certain truth — that modern British Governments can live, or die, by the media: a lesson the present Prime Minister never allows himself to forget. He has done more to woo, flatter and win over the media than any other, I guess: and is reviled for it by ... the media. I am among those who wish the Government would engage more directly in a debate with the media on how the two relate. But we would have to recognize that such a debate is possible only by permission of ... the media. The itch to have power over politicians is a very compelling one, as the purchase price of the Telegraph Group showed — one reason why it is a good thing we have a large publicly-owned broadcaster, which can be held accountable in a way private interests can't.

Another issue, which I think is a vast and largely unexplored terrain, is the way in which public affairs are now described. These are being enfolded more and more by the media. In July 2004, an Australian TV channel — Channel 7—launched a competition to see which six candidates from a televised reality-TV-style competition would be selected by viewers as prospective MPs. The six would actually run for the Australian Senate, their campaign costs paid for by the channel. ITV in this country will follow suit. The walls are tumbling down. This is an extreme. More routinely, politicians are now being enfolded in comedy, satire, drama of every kind: their morality (usually) harshly criticized. The fictionalization of the political terrain, nearly always to the detriment of the politicians, has gone very far. A documentary like *Fahrenheit 9/11*, which makes no attempt to consider arguments other than its own and is wholly opaque about its own arguments, enjoys huge success — as do radio stations of the right, which have the same approach. The weaving of endless tapestries composed of factoids with huge doses of mockery and paranoia produces a public affairs coverage in which the news narrative becomes less and less comprehensible.

The language of politics is increasingly the language of the media. We don't recognize other languages — as of political debate, or the law, or science. It's not just a matter of making things simple: it's about according separate spheres separate languages and customs. Once politicians come into that sphere created by the media — and New Labour certainly did — then they become at least in part its prisoner; and as their novelty fades, so they become an object of increasing contempt. This may be, as Onora O'Neill suggests, a substantial part of the Government's problem over the dossier. It had to be made punchy: how else would it be heard? And thus, in an effort to be heard, Government finds a forest of deaf ears. My interest is not so much saying, yet again, to the politicians that this is their fault, but to ask what have we, the media, done to bring the present situation about? And what can we do to set it right? Or do we think we don't have to?

Lessons for Governmental Process

MICHAEL QUINLAN

The Hutton and Butler inquiries were directly concerned with aspects of the Iraq saga. They were high-profile events in the long public inquisition into the merits — political, legal and moral — of the war into which Mr Blair took the United Kingdom. (It is not unfair to characterize the matter thus, for UK participation was driven by the Prime Minister's personal choice in a degree unmatched, as Peter Hennessy reminds us, since Anthony Eden's role in the 1956 Suez enterprise.) Public commentary on the inquiries naturally concentrated upon their significance in that context, but one may doubt whether in the event they had much effect in changing minds on the fundamental issue — they were not, and politically could not have been, addressed head-on to that. They tidied up the debate usefully, in that they cut the ground from under the wilder suspicions that sinister agents had done away with Dr David Kelly, or that Mr Blair had been both wicked and rash enough to tell downright and deliberate lies about Saddam Hussein's possession of weapons of mass destruction (though there is more to good faith than merely the avoidance of direct mendacity, and indeed the assertion that the evidence was 'extensive, detailed and authoritative' surely skirted the boundaries of that). It had, however, been plain enough well before either inquiry reported, and was thereafter amply confirmed by other means, that the WMD threat had been far more limited and less imminent than was proclaimed — most emphatically by Mr Blair — in advance of the war. No new facts or considerations emerged from either inquiry to shift, other than marginally, the divide already well established between those who believed, with the claims by President Bush and Mr Blair, that the removal of a malign tyrant anyway justified the war and those who believed that neither the principle of this nor the balance of costs incurred did so. The inquiries could, for example, play no part in clarifying the scale of Iraqi deaths, a major factor from

117

which governments on both sides of the Atlantic continued sedulously to avert their gaze.

The two inquiries had, however, interest and significance reaching beyond the Iraq issue, in two main general ways. (I do not here revisit the more specific question, uncomfortably crystallized around the awkward matter of whether Mr John Scarlett should so precipitately have been given advancement as the new Chief of the Secret Intelligence Service while the Butler inquiry was still in progress, of what responsibility in public office ought to entail when things go wrong, as they plainly did within Mr Scarlett's field in more respects than just mistaken intelligence assessment.) First, the inquiries prompted questions about the place of such investigations in British constitutional practice. Second, the unfettered access they were given to people, papers and emails yielded an extraordinarily close and revealing portrait of how contemporary government at the centre of the British system has been functioning.

The use of inquiries

Inquiries by special process had been widely undertaken in recent decades, as for example into the disposal of the body parts of dead children at the Alder Hey Hospital in Liverpool, or the shortcomings of police and local-authority procedures and actions as they bore upon the murder of two schoolgirls at Soham in 2002. The distinctive class into which the Hutton and Butler inquiries fell is, however, that of investigation into the doings of central government in major matters. (The death of Dr Kelly, though in itself a very particular event, was of wider public interest because of the policy context within which it occurred.) Other recent examples of the genre, after the inquiry led by Lord Franks into the origins of the 1982 Falklands War, include the 1992–96

118

investigation by Sir Richard Scott into the supply of military equipment to Iraq, the 1997–2000 review led by Lord Phillips of the debacle over bovine spongiform encephalitis, the long-running scrutiny of the 'Bloody Sunday' happenings which Lord Saville began in 1998, the relatively swift inquiry – not now much remembered – by Sir Thomas Legg and Sir Robin Ibbs in 1998 on the movement of arms into Sierra Leone, and Dr Ian Anderson's 2001 examination of how the foot-and-mouth outbreak was handled. All the issues thus examined had become the subject of heated political argument, and a natural initial question about them as a class is why they could not have been left to be dealt with by Parliament as the prime constitutional forum for the Government's accountability.

The answer seems to lie in three sets of perceived limitations upon Parliament's investigatory effectiveness. One of these concerns credibility. Rightly or wrongly, it is feared that where the standing of the Government as a whole, or of a particular minister, is under challenge, the pressures of party allegiance and interest will impair the rigour with which exploration is pursued or distort the objectivity with which conclusions are reached.

A second perceived source of limitation relates to the powers available for parliamentary investigation. The Hutton, Butler and similar inquiries were given a licence to demand detailed information about Government's inner workings that no major party, at least when in office, has been prepared to concede generally to parliamentary committees. The reason for the difference, against the background of an underlying belief that good government requires the dependable ability to conduct business in private, is an understanding that special inquiries can be given – and generally trusted to adhere to – tightly-defined remits and are conducted by individuals not actuated by the protective or adversarial concerns of elected politicians. The presence of Mrs Ann Taylor and Colonel Michael Mates on the

Butler Committee is an interesting semi-exception to this, but they constituted a minority within the Committee, as did Members of Parliament in the Franks Inquiry; and all these moreover were Privy Counsellors, who had accordingly taken an oath of confidentiality. That status and the constraint it imposes could not easily or regularly be insisted upon in parliamentary committees.

The third perceived limitation relates to resources and skills. In the past 25 years the more systematic framework of Departmental Select Committees has undoubtedly strengthened the ability of the House of Commons to examine what Governments do. Some of the Committees, and individual Members of Parliament within them, have developed considerable expertise — and occasionally a notable independence of party — in that role. It cannot however be expected, amid the diverse demands upon MPs and the exiguous staffing support (both personal and collective) available to them, that they will easily find time for the research and cross-examination needed to get to the root of complicated issues in the depth of detail that we have seen in the Hutton and Butler inquiries. When public confidence is seen as demanding that depth, normal parliamentary process will inevitably be at a disadvantage. That disadvantage is compounded by limitations — again understandable, and interestingly now acknowledged by the House of Commons Liaison Committee — in the armoury of forensic skills which MPs can normally be expected to bring to bear.

On this analysis, three further questions next arise. Are special inquiries actually achieving what we want from them? Should we mind if we find ourselves continuingly or even increasingly impelled to use them for investigations which constitutional theory would ideally assign to Parliament? Can anything be done to ease the parliamentary limitations which are thought to drive us that way?

Achieving the aim? The immediate task of such inquiries is to establish thoroughly what has happened, so as to allay any public fears of cover-up. Beyond that, the careful consultative paper on inquiries published in May 2004 by the Department for Constitutional Affairs stated that 'the primary purpose of an inquiry is to prevent recurrence'[1] and 'the main aim is to learn lessons, not apportion blame'.[2] (One might add to that the value of enhancing deterrence for the future.) But it has to be acknowledged that this is not how public opinion, as voiced or shaped by the media, generally sees matters. There is a sense of need for cathartic lancing of boils; the predominant expectation may be that the 'guilty' will be identified and pilloried, and it is the disappointment of that expectation that prompts accusations of 'whitewash', as it did in respect of the Hutton Inquiry and might still have done even if the report's conclusions had had a little more to say about shortcomings on the Government as well as the BBC side. (The expectation needs nevertheless to recognize that the more salient the 'blame' theme is made within an inquiry, the stronger the pressures become for careful lawyerly process, with all its costs in time and money.) There is no ready escape from this disjuncture between official purpose and popular hope, or from the suspicion that, for Governments, the motivation for setting up inquiries may sometimes have a component of near-term desire to buy time, cool temperatures, and hope for distractions. But none of this makes inquiries bad or useless instruments. Both the Hutton and the Butler reports will have prompted valuable improvements in fields of public concern; and reflection upon their contribution may help deepen, for next time, cumulative understanding of what can and what cannot reasonably be expected from such exercises.

---

[1] *Effective Inquiries: A consultation paper produced by the Department for Constitutional Affairs*, CP 12/04 (May 2004), para. 39, p. 19.

[2] Ibid. para. 82, p. 31.

Should we mind using the inquiry device? We ought perhaps to recognize two grounds for being wary of over-ready recourse to it. One is cost. Even if we set apart, as wholly exceptional, the £155 million expected cost of the Bloody Sunday Inquiry, the figure given for the BSE Inquiry is £26 million and that for the Scott Inquiry £7 million excluding — surely a large exclusion? — the costs of legal aid and Government legal services. These are not trivial demands upon the taxpayer. Beyond this, there may be a less precise but not less important risk that, although in formal terms the inquiries are usually an aid to Parliament and not a substitute for it, their continual use might further erode the authority, experience and practical competence of Parliament's own mechanisms in holding Government to account.

Can Parliament be made more effective, and more commanding of public confidence, in dealing directly with complex and contentious issues? There is no evading the facts of party allegiance and the inhibitions this imposes, especially within a parliamentary as distinct from a separation-of-powers constitutional framework. In addition, it is neither realistic nor desirable that parliamentary committees should be accorded general rights of deep excavation into internal Government process on the scale that Hutton and Butler were enabled to exercise. No executive anywhere could function well under a permanent and comprehensive political shadow of such a kind. Parliamentary limitations might, however, be modestly alleviated by the improved resourcing of staff support, for which there is a case also on other grounds; and it will be interesting to see whether the Liaison Committee's idea of specific training in cross-examination skills is taken up, and whether it makes a difference.

It is tempting to add that Parliament's authority depends also upon its ability to exploit the product of inquiries in discharging its own role as penultimate holder-to-account (the ultimate one being the electorate). Whatever one's view of the merits of the Iraq

122

war, it seemed remarkable that the contribution of ministers in listening to and winding up the 20 July debate on the Butler report in the House of Commons — and indeed the reporting of that debate in the media, including the BBC — apparently felt able to take so little account of the weight of censure powerfully expressed by most speakers from all sides of the House. (Of twenty-three back-bench speakers, twelve of them Labour, only three voiced unequivocal support for the Prime Minister.) The discomfort of a Leader of the Opposition impaled upon the eager support of the war to which his predecessor had committed his party clearly played a major part in that impunity, but the event overall brought home the reality that, however bright and accurate the searchlights, effect in the end rests with the anti-aircraft batteries.

Given that inquiries will continue to be an occasional tool of public audit of central government, do the Hutton and Butler experiences offer any new messages about how they should be constituted and operated? After the Scott Inquiry several commentators argued that its value had been vitiated or at least impaired (quite aside from its near-four-year duration and 1800-page summary-less report) by needlessly adversarial style and failure to comprehend adequately the governmental realities of having to conduct complicated business under pressure of scarce time and diversely-overflowing in-trays. It was suggested *inter alia* that such perceived imperfections in the inquiry could have been eased by the assignment, if not of co-members, at least of weighty assessors able to bring to bear relevant practical background. Lord Hutton also sat alone, but was seen as succeeding in avoiding these pitfalls (though that might perhaps have been less easy if he had interpreted his remit as broadly as some of the subsequent grumbles thought he should have done). The pattern doubtless needs to be weighed case by case, and there are good and bad examples to be found in either direction. It is, however, questionable whether the matter should turn on a fear that the addition of supporting members or assessors will undesirably extend the time taken. That scarcely seems necessarily so (especially in the light of Scott's solitary marathon) and even if it were, the price might be worth paying for higher quality-assurance in the outcome.

William Twining and Michael Beloff differ on the appropriateness of having judges take part in inquiries. To someone from outside the legal world the question 'Who better, on a balance of public interest?' presents itself; and appeal to the United States analogy of customary refusal needs to be qualified by the fact — as we were vividly reminded by the Supreme Court's consideration of the outcome of the 2000 Presidential election — that the US environment provides less public acceptance than does ours of judicial freedom from political bias.

The composition of the Butler Committee was more diverse and less politics-free than had latterly been usual for such inquiries. That inescapably carried potential drawbacks, and it would be surprising if there were no truth at all in media speculation that there had to be bargaining about some of the report's language and conclusions. The report was, however, successfully delivered against a tight deadline without need for minority dissent, and proved by no means unable to say trenchant things likely to be found uncomfortable within Government. That achievement was a tribute to the particular skills and attitudes within the Committee and its support, but served also to encourage retention of its structure and method among options for the future.

The working of Government

The Government wisely felt, as its forerunner had done with the Scott Inquiry, that for reasons both of substance and of public credibility the Hutton and Butler inquiries must be manifestly free to probe without limitation the details of internal Government activity in the relevant field. The result was that both inquiries, in different and complementary ways, yielded an exceptionally unconstrained and unvarnished picture of how the centre of the current Government had been working. A great deal of this, for all that it might raise the eyebrows of the public or the media, came as neither unexpected nor particularly disquieting to anyone who had worked closely in Whitehall across a span of administrations.

There were however significant exceptions to that relaxed recognition. The exposure, in the evidence which Lord Hutton elicited, of the remarkable informality (to use no sharper term) of how business was transacted within No. 10 was surely an uncomfortable surprise even to *cognoscenti*. The Butler Report voiced justifiably adverse comment upon how the relationship had come to function between the intelligence world and key policy-concerned figures in and around No. 10. Most strikingly of all, that report then ended with what was, in its context, a dramatically critical six-paragraph *envoi* about the general way in which Mr Blair had organized and run the collective Cabinet dimension of his leadership.

We should bear in mind the antecedents of the situation revealed. Whenever there is a change after one party has had a long run in office, the incomers are always tempted to suspect that those who worked for their predecessors may be deficient in understanding of or commitment to a new agenda. The neutral mindset of thorough and loyal service redirected as necessary to support whomever the electorate may place in power can seem alien or even incredible to those whose operating context has been the political struggle, perhaps especially younger activists for whom partisan conviction has been the mainspring of action. A particularly protracted period out of office can intensify such attitudes.

Mr Blair was the first Prime Minister since Ramsay MacDonald in 1924 to come to No. 10 without previous experience of his own at any level within Government, and he was surrounded by party colleagues who were mostly little if any better equipped in that regard. It was moreover not immediately obvious that those colleagues embodied an apt range and depth of talent to fill the entire span of Cabinet posts. When Labour had last come to power, Harold Wilson was able to preside over a Cabinet including, for example, Denis Healey, James Callaghan, Anthony Crosland, Roy Jenkins, Barbara Castle and Anthony Benn. It is surely not just nostalgic *laudatio temporis acti* that sees more than merely a difference of experience in the contrast between 1974 and 1997. (In fairness, a similar comparison of other party front benches over time might suggest that the inference to be drawn relates to the condition of British political life and participation, not of one party only.)

Mr Blair thus entered office with limitations both in the resources available to him and in his own feel for the customary running of public business. (Whatever one may think of the balance of might-have-beens in other respects, John Smith — for whom I once worked closely and with trust on both sides upon a project of whose merits he knew I became sceptical — would surely have understood the Government machine more clearly and confidently, and handled issues of structure and procedure differently. But that is alternative history.) Against that background, it is neither surprising nor illegitimate that a Prime Minister of Mr Blair's abilities, energy and self-confidence, coming to and subsequently retaining power moreover with the endorsement of the electorate in exceptional degree, should have chosen to operate in a more centralized way than almost any predecessor, and in doing so should have been keen to reshape working practices in new ways (including swift and determined management of media concerns) which he regarded as more suited to his task and aims than older ones.

It is, however, open to question, as we survey the scene disclosed by Hutton and Butler, whether the changes — often, it seemed, reflecting a marked impatience with collective process — always rested upon sufficient understanding that existing patterns had not been developed without practical reason, and that departing from them might therefore have a downside that needed careful consideration beforehand. Where, as in Britain, there is no written constitution and governmental practice rests largely upon convention rather than entrenched rule or statute, changes may be more easily made than in a more formalized setting; but that does not render thorough, timely and transparent evaluation any the less important. In the governance of a major country, a highly centralized — even personalized — system of work may moreover be in extra need of careful method and record.

The absence of thorough analysis, and of a system for conducting it, had already been conspicuously displayed in the near-shambles surrounding the attempt to abolish the post of Lord Chancellor; but Hutton and Butler in combination suggested that the effects might run more widely. It was increasingly to be suspected that Mr Blair's administration had often had little interest in or tolerance for distinctions of function and responsibility between different categories of actor within the Government machine (except perhaps when political defences needed to be erected, as over the purported 'ownership' of the September 2002 dossier). Not only in the interface with the intelligence structure and in the way Alastair Campbell operated within and beyond No. 10, but also in matters such as the saga of Jo Moore and Martin Sixsmith in the Department of Transport, there was a sense of all participants — ministers, civil servants, special policy advisers, public relations handlers — being treated as part of an undifferentiated resource for the support of the central executive. Flexibility and a fostering of 'all-of-one-company' goal-oriented spirit are of course assets, and to make a fetish of role-demarcation does not serve the public interest. Ignoring professional boundaries, however, carries a temptation to — or may be a reflection of — lack of consistent and dependable system; and that was the impression left by some of what the Hutton and Butler reports disclosed.

Mr Blair has sought to bring to his Prime Ministership a strong focus upon delivery — the achievement of practical results. This salutary concern can, however, slide into a sense that outcome is the only true reality and that process is flummery. But the two are not antithetical, still less inimical to one another. Process is care and thoroughness; it is consultation, involvement and co-ownership; it is (as we were reminded by the failure of international process in the run-up to the Iraq war) legitimacy and acceptance; it is also record, auditability and clear accountability. It is often accordingly a significant component of outcome itself; and the more awkward and demanding the issue — especially amid the special gravity of peace and war — the more it may come to matter.

The closing paragraphs of the Butler Report, remarkable enough in themselves, were made more so by the facts both that their inclusion represented something of a stretch of the Committee's remit, and that the Committee's composition meant that they carried the assent of Mrs Ann Taylor, who had been a participant in Mr Blair's Cabinet. Mr Blair swiftly indicated his intention to make adjustments in the light of the report, but it was not immediately apparent whether he would choose — or be induced by Cabinet colleagues — to carry these far enough to constitute a real change of approach. Cabinet government of the traditional model has manifestly atrophied over the past seven years, and moreover by deliberate neglect, not accident. Should we mind? If a collective Cabinet system no longer functions well, and Parliament is in practice docile or impotent, we may be nearer to 'elective dictatorship' than when Lord Hailsham's coining of that phrase, a quarter of a century ago, was widely dismissed as hyperbole. Perhaps the country is content that the media should be left as the prime constraint upon highly-centralized power. But the issues surely deserve public discussion.

Tests of whether Mr Blair truly intends reformation might include whether opportunities are to be exploited, as personnel changes arise, to revive the full scope and authority of the Cabinet Secretary post (to an observer from yesteryear the invisibility of the incumbent during the events recounted by Hutton and Butler was striking) and to restore the focus of the Secretariat upon support of the Cabinet as a whole. Another test, even if its immediate impact be modest, might be the serious pursuit of a Civil Service Act to entrench certain basic safeguards. In an age where established convention mostly (and healthily) commands less ready reverence than in the past, it may well be appropriate that roles, procedures and systems be more explicitly defined, even if sometimes only by administrative instrument, than used to be thought necessary. That may be the more desirable given the possibility, increasing as time passes, that the next change of Government may again bring into office a team with no more than limited and distant experience.

The remedying of what went amiss, whether through misjudgement or oversight, matters accordingly for reasons stretching beyond the further life (even if it be a long one) of the present Government. Governing parties are more than just tenants of the constitutional structure; they have a right, even a duty, to modify it where they judge that the people will thus be better served (though any such modification ought to be made openly, with proper discussion and accountability). But they remain less than owners; they are more like trustees, with an obligation to maintain the structure and hand it on to eventual successors in good working order. The Hutton and Butler scrutinies in effect called into question whether the obligation was being fully secured. On that showing, Mr Blair and his proper advisers had repair work to do, and to demonstrate.

About the British Academy

The British Academy, established by Royal Charter in 1902, is the UK's national academy for the humanities and the social sciences, the counterpart to the Royal Society which exists to serve the physical and biological sciences.

The Academy is an independent learned society, a self-governing body of Fellows elected in recognition of their distinction as scholars in a branch of the humanities or the social sciences.

With the help of a Government grant-in-aid, the Academy sponsors and funds research; it represents the humanities and social sciences nationally and internationally; and it organizes wide-ranging programmes to sustain and disseminate advanced research, and to enhance appreciation of the humanities and social sciences and their contributions to the intellectual, cultural, social and economic well-being of the nation.